Christian Heroes: Then & Now

WILLIAM BOOTH

Soup, Soap, and Salvation

Christian Heroes: Then & Now

WILLIAM BOOTH

Soup, Soap, and Salvation

JANET & GEOFF BENGE

YWAM Publishing is the publishing ministry of Youth With A Mission (YWAM), an international missionary organization of Christians from many denominations dedicated to presenting Jesus Christ to this generation. To this end, YWAM has focused its efforts in three main areas: (1) training and equipping believers for their part in fulfilling the Great Commission (Matthew 28:19), (2) personal evangelism, and (3) mercy ministry (medical and relief work).

For a free catalog of books and materials, call (425) 771-1153 or (800) 922-2143. Visit us online at www.ywampublishing.com.

William Booth: Soup, Soap, and Salvation

Sixth printing 2021

Published by YWAM Publishing
a ministry of Youth With A Mission
P.O. Box 55787, Seattle, WA 98155-0787

ISBN 978-1-57658-258-9 (paperback)
ISBN 978-1-57658-598-6 (ebook)

Printed in the United States of America

Christian Heroes: Then & Now

Adoniram Judson
Albert Schweitzer
Amy Carmichael
Betty Greene
Brother Andrew
Cameron Townsend
Charles Mulli
Clarence Jones
Corrie ten Boom
Count Zinzendorf
C. S. Lewis
C. T. Studd
David Bussau
David Livingstone
Dietrich Bonhoeffer
D. L. Moody
Elisabeth Elliot
Eric Liddell
Florence Young
Francis Asbury
George Müller
Gladys Aylward
Helen Roseveare
Hudson Taylor
Ida Scudder
Isobel Kuhn
Jacob DeShazer
Jim Elliot
John Flynn
John Newton
John Wesley
John Williams
Jonathan Goforth
Klaus-Dieter John
Lillian Trasher
Loren Cunningham
Lottie Moon
Mary Slessor
Mildred Cable
Nate Saint
Norman Grubb
Paul Brand
Rachel Saint
Richard Wurmbrand
Rowland Bingham
Samuel Zwemer
Sundar Singh
Wilfred Grenfell
William Booth
William Carey

Available in paperback, e-book, and audiobook formats. Unit study curriculum guides are available for select biographies.

www.YWAMpublishing.com

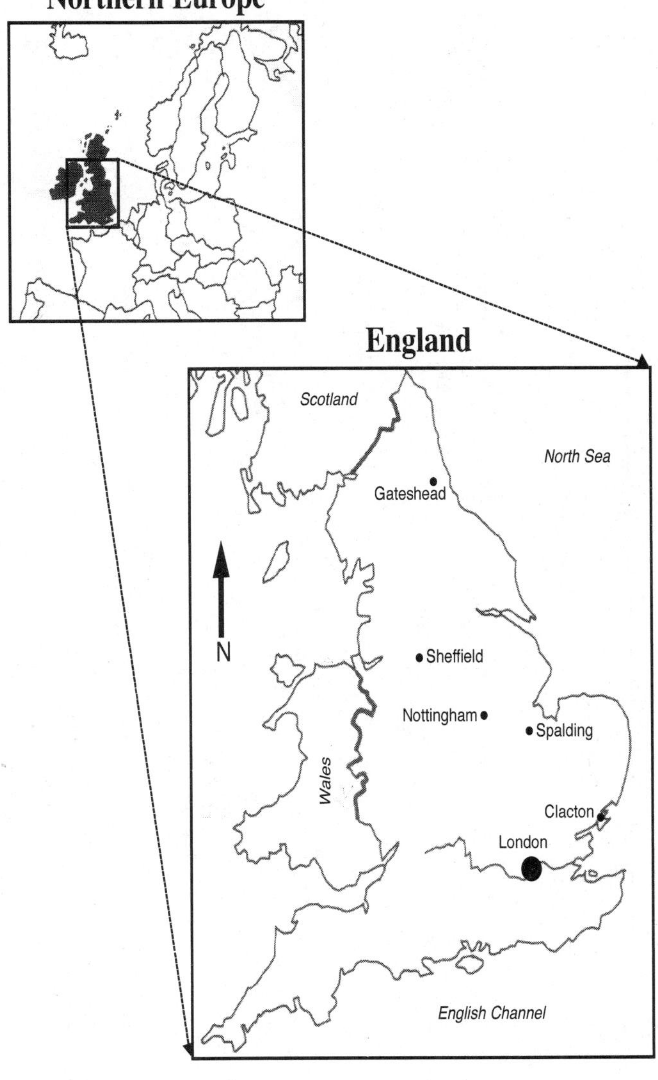

Northern Europe
England
Scotland
North Sea
Gateshead
N
Sheffield
Nottingham
Spalding
Wales
Clacton
London
English Channel

Contents

Chapter 1

A Thorn in the Flesh

"Ahhheeeeee!!! Ahhheeeeee!!!" Elizabeth Geikie, a pretty, blue-eyed woman with a dark complexion from Dundee, Scotland, raced out of her tiny mud hut in the jungle near the village of Alady in Nagercoil, India, to see where the bloodcurdling noise was coming from. It was coming from the path that led to her dwelling.

Soon a group of men from Alady were approaching her hut. They carried a man who was the source of all the noise. At first Elizabeth thought he might be crazy and the villagers were bringing him to torment her. She waited anxiously as the group stopped in front of her hut and laid the man at her feet.

"This man has something wrong, and we don't know what to do," one of the men in the group said.

Elizabeth soon learned that the man was not mad at all but was wailing from excruciating pain. But what was the source of the pain? Had he eaten poison or been bitten by a cobra? She knelt down and began to inspect his body for clues to the pain. It was then that she noticed his left foot was swollen. She touched it, and the man let out another blood-curdling yell. Gingerly she inspected the foot, where she found the source of the pain—a small point protruding from the sole. It was the end of a huge, embedded thorn.

From the hut Elizabeth fetched her medical kit, but inside it she found only petroleum jelly, Epsom salts, and castor oil, and not the forceps she needed to extract the thorn from the man's foot. She would have to improvise.

To the horror of those gathered around, Elizabeth knelt down, leaned forward, and placed her lips against the dirty, callused sole of the man's foot. She then clamped her white teeth around the protruding end of the thorn and slowly moved her head back. Bit by bit the embedded thorn began to slide out of the foot until her head jerked back and the thorn was out. Immediately the man let out a cry of relief as his agonizing pain began to subside.

With the thorn extracted, Elizabeth bathed the wound in coconut oil and then wrapped a lint bandage around it. Soon the man and the group that had brought him disappeared as quickly as they had arrived.

The next day the group of men were back. This time they did not have another injured person with them. Instead they wanted answers.

"Why is it that you, a white woman, would want to save the life of a man by placing your lips, the most sacred part of the body, against his foot, the most despised part of the body?"

"Because my God, who loves and values all men, asked me to do it," she replied.

This was the opening Elizabeth Geikie had been praying for, and soon those in the group were clamoring to know more about her God.

First the man from whose foot she had extracted the thorn and his wife became Christian converts. Soon others from the village followed, until the nucleus of a small church had been formed.

William Booth laid the report from India that contained Elizabeth Geikie's story on his desk and walked to his office window. As he looked out at the brick and stone facades of London's buildings, a smile of satisfaction settled across his face. Elizabeth's action was the kind of selfless demonstration of the power of the gospel that touched people and changed their hearts. Her action was more powerful than the words of any sermon. Despite the vicious persecution members of the Salvation Army had endured since setting foot in India, Elizabeth was a woman who would not allow the message of God's love to be silenced.

Elizabeth had done what William and any other member of the Salvation Army would have done. They would have shown God's love in whatever practical way possible. In the very streets of London below, people were out doing the same thing at that moment, helping the poor and needy, comforting the sick and the weak, and bringing the hope of God's love into otherwise hopeless lives and situations.

That is what William Booth had striven to do all his life. From the first time he encountered those on the fringes of society in his hometown of Nottingham, he had been drawn like a magnet to them and their needs. They were the people God had given him to minister the gospel to, and now a vast army of people like Elizabeth Geikie was spread around the world doing the same.

William sank back into the chair behind his desk to continue reading the dispatch from India. Before he could pick up the paper, he found his thoughts wandering back to Nottingham, where it had all begun.

Chapter 2

"Always Seek the Advantage"

William Booth raced across the cobblestone street, leaping over a large, muddy puddle. The bell was just being rung as he reached the bottom step to Biddulph's School for Young Gentlemen. Before he mounted the steps, William glanced down to make sure his jacket buttons were properly fastened and there was no mud on his shoes. As he did so, he spied a small leather pouch lying beneath the hedge. He walked over and picked it up. Inside were three coins—a shilling and two sixpences. William whistled to himself; it was a lot of money. He stuffed the pouch and the money into his trouser pocket. He would have to think carefully about how he might spend it.

All the other ten-year-old boys in his class were standing in line when William finally made it up the stairs and into the hallway. He quickly joined the end of the line, trying to make himself as inconspicuous as possible. This was difficult, however, since he was tall for his age—a good head and shoulders above anyone else in the class.

Soon the boys were all seated at their desks. As they recited Latin phrases, William's attention wandered, and he began to stare out the window. It was a gray, overcast day in 1839, and Nottingham looked as drab and uninviting as ever. In the grimy, dank street below, a young girl holding a crying baby wandered by, followed by a coal merchant on a cart pulled by a scraggly, emaciated horse.

A ruler rapped on William's desk. "I doubt you have listened to a word I've said, Mr. Booth!" the teacher exploded. "Students who do not listen in class fail in their homework. Tomorrow I shall be paying close attention to the work you do at home tonight." With that the teacher dismissed the class for lunch.

William stuffed his books in his bag and joined the other boys leaving the classroom. "I think I'm in trouble now," he said, half smiling to his best friend, Robert Powell.

"You'll get through it; you always do," Robert replied, and then his face darkened. "Besides, you don't really have a problem compared to Harry and me."

"What do you mean?" William asked.

"My mother gave me money this morning to pay our school fees. I know I put it in my pocket, but when I got to school the money was gone. I don't know what I'm going to do. My father will whip me when I tell him."

"My father would do the same to me!" William agreed. Then a thought flashed through his mind. He reached into his pocket and felt the money pouch. "Was the money in anything?" he asked.

"A small leather pouch," Robert replied. "But there's no use looking for it. Even if I knew where I dropped it, someone would have found it by now."

William's hand closed around the pouch in his pocket, but something stopped him from pulling it out. He heard the echo of his father's voice: "Always seek the advantage, lad, always seek the advantage."

So what should William do in this situation? He knew he would give the money back to Robert. It belonged to Robert, and William could not keep it knowing that. But *how* should he give it back? Should he just say, "Here, I found this?" or think of some other way to return the money that gave him an advantage over Robert and his brother Harry?

William released the pouch and pulled his empty hand out of his pocket. Patting Robert on the back he said, "Don't worry. There'll be some way out of this. I'll help you."

By the time lunch was nearly over, William knew what he would do. He put his soupspoon down and turned to his friend. "Robert, I have been thinking about how bad it would be to go home and tell your mother you lost the money. It just so happens that I have two shillings in my bag. I have been saving it up for a year. I was going to use it to buy myself a model train, but I don't see how I can do that now, since my best friend is in need." He reached into his pocket and emptied the coins out of the pouch. He then pulled the coins from his pocket. "Here, you take them," he said.

"But I couldn't," Robert said, his eyes wide with surprise. "Really, I couldn't. It's such a lot of money. I never knew you had so much saved."

"You must take it," William said, putting the coins on the table between them. "If you don't, you and Harry will both get a thrashing."

"I'll think of a way to pay you back. Honest I will!" Robert said as he scooped up the money.

William finished his soup with a sense of quiet satisfaction. His father would be proud of him. He had found a way to give the money back while getting the advantage.

Before they went home from school that night, Robert thrust something into William's hand. "Here," he said, "take this. My uncle brought it back from India for us, but I want you to have it, to say thank you."

William looked down. There in his hand was Robert Powell's pride and joy—a shiny sterling silver pencil case. He hesitated for a moment. Should he tell Robert the whole truth? No, it was too late now. Besides, he had always admired the pencil case.

"Thank you," William mumbled without looking up. "I have to go now."

As William walked over the bridge on his way home that evening, he threw the empty money pouch into the River Trent. On the other side of the river he noticed that a makeshift scaffold had been set up and a huge crowd had gathered around it. He stopped at the edge of the crowd to see what was happening.

"He deserves everything he gets!" an old woman said to a man in a baker's hat and apron.

"That he does," the baker replied. "Imagine, he killed his wife and children. Whatever he gets is too good for him."

As William climbed halfway up a gaslight pole for a better look, a man was marched out onto the scaffold. A cheer went up from the crowd, and mothers held up their young children for a better look. A bag was placed over the man's head, and then the man was dragged over to the hanging noose. As the crowd went wild with excitement, William felt his stomach turn. He did not want to be there. He did not want to see a man die with the echo of a cheering crowd in his ears.

Quickly William climbed down the gaslight pole and slipped into a side street. Tears streamed down his face as he raced to get as far away from the crowd as he could. He was glad to get home to his mother.

"What's the matter?" Mary Booth asked as he came in the door. "You look as white as a sheet!"

William sat down at the kitchen table and began telling his mother what he had seen.

"Hush," she said. "Don't say another word in front of the little ones." She then turned and addressed William's two younger sisters. "Emma, Mary, you two go upstairs and put away your dolls."

When they had gone, William continued recounting his story. He was nearly finished when his older sister, twelve-year-old Ann, burst into the room. "Mother," she said, "have you heard the awful news? There was a riot at the hanging today. The crowd kept pushing closer and closer to the scaffolding until it gave way. Twelve people were crushed to death. Twelve people! They say one of them was Mr. Jamieson, our bootmaker."

Mary Booth got up and put her arms around her daughter. "God help us," she said. "The world is becoming a more brutal place every day. Imagine twelve people losing their lives trying to get a better view of such an awful sight."

Following that event-filled day, things returned to the mundane for William Booth. During the week he attended school, and on the weekends he helped his father, Samuel, with his house-building job.

The following year Mr. Biddulph, William's schoolmaster, invited the students to attend a meeting at the Broad Street Chapel in Nottingham. This was a Methodist church started three years before, in 1837. Everyone talked about how huge the building was inside. It had enough seats for two thousand people. William's father told him it had cost the enormous sum of eleven thousand pounds to buy the land and build the church.

As William stood outside staring up at the four columns that formed the colonnade at the front of the church, he wondered what the service inside would be like. Until now William had attended St. Stephen's Anglican Church with his mother and three sisters. His father seldom attended the church, and William understood why. The minister stood in a pulpit high above the congregation and preached using such big words that William could understand little of what was said. And his voice droned on so that William had to fight to stay awake.

The service at Broad Street Chapel was astoundingly different from anything else William had experienced. The preacher read from the Bible and then, using simple words and ideas, carefully explained the meaning of the passage. As he spoke, people in the congregation yelled out, "Praise the Lord" and "Hallelujah." William could hardly believe it. A person would be removed from St. Stephen's for yelling at the preacher! And the singing amazed him, too. He had never heard such hymns before—so full of joy and action. They made him want to get up and march around the room! And the way prayers were said was also totally foreign to William. Instead of reading from page sixty-two of the Prayer Book, people just spoke out their own prayers, made up right there on the spot. By the time the service was over, William knew one thing for sure: This was the liveliest church he had ever experienced, and he was going to come back as often as he could for services.

The summer of 1842 was one William would never forget. It was the summer in which his father lost all of the family's money. The man who had always encouraged William to "seek the advantage" made one shaky deal too many, and the family was ruined financially. There was no way William could continue attending school; it was much too expensive. Besides, he was now thirteen years old—old enough to get a job and contribute to the family income.

Within days William's clothes were packed and he was sent off to work for Francis Eames. Mr. Eames was a pawnbroker in Goosegate, Nottingham, and William was to be his apprentice for five years. This meant that William would live above the pawnshop and learn the trade of pawnbrokering. The sudden change in his circumstances shocked William, but he realized there was little he could do about it. His father was in charge of him, and he had no choice but to obey him.

William began to learn the ways of the pawnbroker. The idea was simple, really. Customers brought in items, and Mr. Eames assessed the value of the items and paid the customer about sixty percent of what they were worth. Then he held the items for two weeks. If the customer did not come to buy the items back, he sold them at a profit. Of course, most of the customers were hopeful, even confident, that in two weeks' time they would have the money to redeem their belongings, but few of them did.

William's first job was to sweep the floor and fold the clothes and bedding that people pawned. This was not hard to master, though he had to constantly be on the lookout for ticks and lice that crawled out of the blankets. Soon Mr. Eames promised William that he would show him how to decide what an item was worth and how to extract the most money from the transaction.

This is just the job my father would enjoy—taking advantage of people in their weakest moments, William thought to himself as he folded and swept. But William could not enjoy the "game." He was too concerned about the customers and what they would do next. Some men became wretched enough to pawn the tools of their trade: the carpenter's level and saw, a bricklayer's trowel, or a butcher's knives. William wondered how they would ever get on their feet again without a way to make a living.

Just about all the customers who sought out the pawnshop, with its three brass balls hanging over the doorway, lived in quiet desperation. Often the same customers came back time after time to pawn more of their or their family's possessions for cash to put food on the table or pay the rent on the pitiful hovels they lived in.

Over time William began to see that there was a pattern to the way people pawned things. The first time he met new customers they brought in such items as umbrellas, articles of clothing, and furniture. But as time went by, these same people began bringing in more and more necessary items, such as plates, teapots, and tools, until finally they came wanting to pawn their wedding rings.

Although William felt sorry about the plight of these people, things were also going from bad to worse for the Booth family. In September William's father died. At sixty-eight years of age, he was an old man by the standards of the day, and his marriage to William's mother, Mary, was his second marriage. His first wife and child had died long ago.

William hardly knew how to feel about his father's death. Samuel Booth had always been a distant man, pushing William to make deals and get ahead in the world, two things William felt uneasy about. It was his mother to whom he was most attached. She was the one who encouraged him and told him that one day things would get better.

With her husband's death, William's mother set up a tiny shop not far from the pawnbrokers in Goosegate. William's three sisters became the shop assistants. The shop sold sewing needles, thread, hatpins, handkerchiefs, and other small items that women needed. Whenever she could, Mary Booth slipped into Eames Pawnbrokers to find out how William was faring.

On Sundays William sometimes went to St. Stephen's Church with his mother and sisters, but more often than not he walked the extra distance to Broad Street Chapel. He had grown to love this church, especially the chance to listen to the outstanding preachers who spoke there. Two of them, the Reverend James Caughey from the United States and Yorkshire man Isaac Marsden, particularly inspired him. Something about their preaching drew him like a magnet. Sometimes, after hearing a stirring sermon, William would wander off to Wilford Meadows and try preaching to himself. He was always disappointed with the results, though. The famous preachers he heard at Broad Street Chapel were powerful and articulate. There was something else about them—they spoke with fiery conviction. It was obvious they believed what they were preaching with all their heart. William, on the other hand, was not sure what he believed.

Even though he had been going to this church for two years, William was still a "spectator." He enjoyed the free-flowing atmosphere there, the lively singing, and the preaching, but he had never settled the matter about the state of his own soul. It seemed an enormous decision to give his life wholly to God in the way that the Methodist preachers encouraged their listeners to do.

That was the case until one night late in 1844, when fifteen-year-old William Booth strolled into Bible class. The teacher, Henry Carey, opened with the words, "A soul dies every minute." For some reason these words penetrated right into William's heart. What if he died? Where would his soul go? Did he truly belong to Jesus Christ, or was he going to spend the rest of his life dabbling around the edges of Christianity? As William pondered these questions, a thought rushed through his mind. *God shall have all there is of William Booth.*

Henry Carey continued speaking to the Bible class, but William was scarcely aware of what his teacher was saying. The thought played over and over in his mind. Finally, as the class drew to a close, Henry Carey announced, "If anyone would like to own his sins and surrender his life to God, he may meet me at the back of the room."

Without hesitation William leaped from his seat and hurried to the back. He knelt at a wooden table and poured out his thoughts to God. Almost immediately Robert Powell's silver pencil case came to mind. William had felt guilty about having it from the day he tricked Robert with the lost money. Now he knew he had to do something about it. He prayed, "God, I promise I will return the pencil case to Robert as soon as I can." Then he stopped and thought for a moment and then went on, "And I will even tell him how I tricked him into giving it to me."

As William spoke these words, he felt a huge weight lift from his mind. He no longer had to seek the advantage in every deal. There was something much more important to seek now—God's will.

William felt lighter than air that night as he walked back to Eames Pawnshop. He might be a lowly apprentice, but he was determined to give his life—every bit of it—to God. Of course he didn't have the least idea what God would do with his life.

Chapter 3

William's People

That lighthearted feeling did not desert William in the days following his experience at Broad Street Chapel. In fact, he felt even lighter after he found Robert Powell, apologized for tricking him with the money, and gave his silver pencil case back. William also found he was more patient with the customers at the pawnshop and was always ready to quote a few words from the Bible to comfort them. Sometimes he even invited them to attend church, though most people just shook their head or laughed in his face. William longed to do something more effective to share the gospel with these people, but if they refused to come to church with him, what else was there? Two years passed before an opportunity to branch out in evangelizing presented itself.

One winter's day in 1846, seventeen-year-old William Booth lay ill in bed. His fever had gone down some, and the doctor told him he would get better as long as he rested. Resting was not an easy assignment for such an active young man, but as he lay there, William thought a lot about his commitment to give his whole life to God. But what could a seventeen-year-old apprentice do that would make any kind of difference in the world? He did not have the freedom to train to become a pastor, and besides, he did not like reading and studying much. Nor did he have the money to help the poor people who came through the doors of the pawnshop every day. Just as William was beginning to despair that his Christian commitment would never amount to much, there came a knock at the door. His friend Bill Sansom opened it and strolled in.

"I hear you've been through a rough patch," Bill said in his usual cheerful manner. "I brought a pudding my mother baked for you. But if you're not well enough to eat it, I'll take it back. My mother's the best cook in town, you know!"

William grinned. Bill had a way of making a person see the brighter side of things. "Leave it here!" William replied, grinning. "I'm on the mend. The doctor says the worst is over. All I have to do is to get strong again, and I think a good pudding will help."

"I know something else that would help," Bill said. "Some of us boys from the Bible class have decided to form a club and start preaching in the poorest parts of the city. Why don't you join us? It would give you a reason to get back on your feet, and I know you'd be good at it. After all, half the people we are going to preach to probably visit your pawnshop at least once a week. How about it? What do you say?"

"Well, yes, all right," William replied, astonished that an opportunity to make a difference had just presented itself. "As soon as I'm well enough, I'll join you. I take it you preach on Sunday afternoons."

"And in the evenings. I'll tell the other lads to be expecting you, if not next week then the week after. I'd better go now. I have to deliver a spool of Belgian lace to one of my father's customers."

After Bill had left, William lay back in his bed and thought. He knew it was a sin to envy anyone, but it was hard not to envy Bill. He came from a well-to-do family; his father was an importer of fashionable Belgian lace. Better still, Bill had such an easy way with people; "a natural leader" was how others described him. When he suggested an activity, the other boys automatically followed him, even into the slums. William wished he were like that, but he lacked the confidence to encourage others to follow his example.

Two weeks later William joined the other boys from the Bible class. They called themselves "The Mission," and under Bill Sansom's leadership, they marched into the slums to share the gospel. Most people ignored them, a few men cursed them, a small child sat beside them for a while chewing on a mutton bone, and an old washerwoman put down her load and listened while she got up the strength to trudge on. It was not a stunning beginning, but the boys continued to go back week after week, until they had established a regular meeting in a widow's cottage on Kid Street. Near the end of the year, it was William's turn to speak at the service held there.

William was nervous as he stood to preach inside the cottage. His hands shook as he placed his Bible beside two candles on a wooden box that doubled as the pulpit. He was grateful that the only light in the room came from those two candles. Perhaps no one would see just how tense he was.

He took a moment to look around the room into the darkened corners. Everything was grimy. Even the newly washed clothes that hung on the line strung above the fireplace were torn and stained. *They're not even worth a penny at the pawnshop,* he thought to himself. He then surveyed the people who had turned out to hear him speak. There were no men in the room—only the boys from The Mission; several women, each of whom had brought something to sit on; and small children, who squirmed in the women's laps. William took a deep breath, picked up his Bible, and launched into the first sermon he had ever preached to an audience.

Despite the bleak surroundings, the people in the room were friendly and warm. Most were new converts, and they all listened eagerly as William spoke to them and admonished them not to get discouraged when things did not go as they planned or when they fell back into old patterns of behavior. He told them that in their Christian life, like a young child learning to walk, they must get up and keep going.

As the meeting drew to a close, William noticed that Bill had not shown up. This was unusual. Bill was always there. William asked one of the other boys if he knew where Bill was.

"He's sick," the young man replied.

The following afternoon, when William went to visit Bill, he was shocked by what he saw. Bill lay in bed, his eyes unfocused, his pillow drenched with sweat.

"Don't go too near him," Mrs. Sansom whispered. "The doctor is sure he has consumption."

William turned to look at Bill's mother. Her eyes were filled with tears. "Consumption?" he stuttered. "How long has he had it?"

Mrs. Sansom looked away. "It started with a cold about a week ago," she said. "At first we didn't think much of it, but then Bill's condition kept getting worse. He hasn't eaten for days."

William looked down at his friend. "Bill," he said gently, "do you hear me?"

Bill moved his head slightly.

"Then I'm going to pray, and you join me in your thoughts."

When William had finished praying, Mrs. Sansom showed him out of the room. "His father and I hope he will benefit from some sea air," she said. "We are taking him down to the Isle of Wight tomorrow. He's a strong boy, and the doctor says he has as good a chance as anyone at making a full recovery."

That night and every night for the next three months William prayed for his friend, but the awful news came anyway. Bill Sansom had died.

As the news of Bill's death spread, something happened that surprised William. The other boys in The Mission began looking to him for direction and leadership. At first it felt awkward, stepping into his dead friend's shoes, but soon William's confidence grew, and he began to see opportunities for "his boys" to preach everywhere.

Not long after William took over his new responsibilities, a young girl who had been a firm supporter of the Kid Street cottage meeting died. William was determined to make the funeral a celebration of her hope of eternal life. He organized The Mission boys to accompany her body to the graveyard with singing and cries of "Hallelujah!" When the pastor finished delivering a few words at the graveside, William stepped forward and preached a rousing sermon on the joys of knowing God forever.

This approach to presenting the gospel raised many eyebrows, but William did not care. The whole experience had exhilarated him. He had found what he had been looking for—his calling in life.

Soon after the funeral William had the opportunity to preach to one of the most notorious drunks in the slums. His name was Besom Jack, a drunken broom seller. Besom Jack had a terrible temper, often flying into a fit of rage and beating his wife and children for no apparent reason. He spent all his earnings on drink, leaving his wife to scrape together a living for herself and the children by recycling used tea leaves, which she collected from the scullery maids who worked for wealthy families. She then dried the leaves, added green coloring to make them look like "new," and resold them to her poor neighbors.

William had been told that no one except the publican had any time for Besom Jack. So when the man fell to his knees yelling, "God, forgive me, for I am a terrible sinner!" an unnatural hush fell over the street corner where William had been preaching. William got down on his knees beside Besom Jack and led the new convert in a prayer. It was an amazing moment in William's life, and William was soon convinced that his new friend was serious about his commitment to leave his sins behind.

As the weeks went by, other men in the slums were so shocked by the changes in Besom Jack that they too stopped to listen to William preach. Soon they found themselves kneeling on the hard cobblestones to ask God's forgiveness.

All of this presented William with a problem, one he had never really anticipated. What should The Mission do with all of the converts? Many of them did not know how to read, and they had little idea of how to go about living a Christian life. William urged them to attend church and Bible study, but they were reluctant to do so.

"We don't have anything to wear 'cept what we got on," Besom Jack's wife told William. "And there ain't nobody wants us to show up on Sunday lookin' like this—or smellin' like it either," she cackled.

"Nonsense!" William retorted. "What does it matter what you wear to church? Jesus spent much of His time on earth with the poor and needy. He said He came to call the sinner, not the righteous. If He didn't worry about how sinners looked, why should people in the church?"

"I ain't so sure," commented a man who was picking a scab on his neck. "I don't rightly think we belong with the likes of them in church. I ain't never been to church before, and I don't reckon it'd be smart to go anytime soon."

William sighed. What could he say to convince these people that since they had become Christians, the members of Broad Street Chapel were now their brothers and sisters in Christ? It was quite a problem, but William did not give up easily. Eventually he persuaded a group of men and women to go with him to church one Sunday morning.

The group met together in The Bottoms, Nottingham's most notorious slum. From there they made their way to Broad Street Chapel. The service had just begun when they arrived. The Reverend Samuel Dunn was leading the congregation in singing a hymn when William swung the church door open and beckoned the procession to the front of the church, where many of the "rented pews" were empty. He watched as hundreds of pairs of eyes focused on the disheveled people filing into the church. Their clothes were ragged, dirty, and torn, and a pungent odor followed the group in. In his youthful naivete William was sure they would be welcomed. He watched helplessly as his hopes were dashed. The wife of a fishmonger was still wearing her leather apron with blood smeared on it and fish scales stuck to it. William's heart sank as he watched the banker's wife make a show of getting a handkerchief from her purse and holding it over her nose. As the fishmonger's wife plunked herself down in a velvet-cushioned pew, the other people in the pew slid as far away from her as they could.

Resolutely William brought up the rear, making sure that no one in the group slipped away before entering the church. Once everyone had found a seat, William took his place on a pew and heartily joined in singing the hymn with the rest of the congregation. Although the congregation had not given the group a warm welcome, William felt sure that things would improve, particularly if the sermon was about loving others more than yourself, or something like that.

During the service, there were no major incidents, just a few smelly children climbing on their mothers and one retarded man who yelled out every so often. When the service was over, William waited for members of the Broad Street Chapel congregation to come over and greet the men and women from Nottingham's slums. But no one came near them. Some of the women, still holding handkerchiefs over their noses, simply hurried out the door while their husbands glared at William. The only person to talk to William was the Reverend Dunn, who asked to see William in the rectory.

William made sure all of the people he had brought were safely out of the church and headed in the right direction home before he went to meet the Reverend Dunn. He knocked on the rectory door. When it opened, William saw five church deacons, including Bill Sansom's father, waiting for him.

"Sit down, lad, and let's get straight to the point," the Reverend Dunn said with his usual candor. "We all understand that you have a passion for preaching on the streets, but it is not appropriate to bring the riffraff off the streets and seat them beside us in our pews. Rented pews no less. You know that prominent families in town pay good money to have those particular seats available for their use each Sunday."

"Here, here," interjected the church secretary. "It's going to take some time to get the smell out of the building, and I think all of the drapes will have to be washed. That's quite an expense just to have a few drunkards listen to a sermon."

William opened his mouth to speak and then shut it again. He expected the church leaders to welcome new faces, even if members of the congregation were less enthusiastic. What could he say?

The Reverend Dunn spoke in a more soothing tone. "None of us doubt that your heart was in the right place, and these people should have a place to worship, if they do in fact understand what worship means. But it is not appropriate to burden this congregation with so many of them at once. Do you think you could bring them in smaller groups? No one would object if they came in the back door and sat behind the curtain. They couldn't see the service of course, but they could hear it. That would resolve the problem nicely."

"Except for the smell," the church secretary chimed in. "You must get them to change into some clean clothes and bathe before they come. That fish smell is unbearable. I don't think I'll ever eat cod again without being reminded of it!"

"How can you expect them to come in their Sunday best?" William asked, finally finding his voice. "They don't have any Sunday best. Many of them have only the clothes on their backs. And as for bathing, there is only one water pump for every fifty or so hovels, and sometimes it pumps for only twenty minutes a day. They can barely keep themselves in drinking water. They certainly don't have the luxury of a bath."

William grew more desperate as he looked into the deacons' stony faces. "Look, they are doing the best they can. Most of them live on a pittance, having barely enough bread and gruel for one meal a day. Some of the ones I brought today, like Besom Jack, have hardly been sober for a whole day in their lives. They need to be encouraged to follow God and find decent employment. Then they will be able to buy Sunday clothes."

Mr. Sansom sighed. "I see your point, son, and I am in sympathy with you. However, you must remember that the congregation here pays the preacher and the bills. If they all leave on account of your riffraff overrunning the place, there will be no church for any of us to come to. Can't you be content with leaving them in their own surroundings and preaching to them in your cottage meetings?"

William looked from one face to the next, hoping to see some glimmer of encouragement. There was none. He took a deep breath and then spoke. "You have made your wishes very plain. I am sorry that you are troubled by new converts. However, I doubt you will see them again anyway. It was very difficult to convince them that they would be welcome in a proper church, and I see they were right and I was wrong. Good day to you, sirs."

With that William stood up and walked out. He kept walking for most of the afternoon, in fact. At first he was angry with what the deacons and the Reverend Dunn had said to him, but then he began to understand the enormity of what he had asked them all to do. Because he worked in a pawnshop, William was used to seeing the outcasts of society—women carrying smelly children on their hips, men with whiskey heavy on their breath, barely able to prop themselves up at the counter, and young boys who needed to be watched every moment to prevent them from stealing items from the shop. These were William's people, but he had to admit they were not everyone else's people. Somehow he would have to find a way to break down the barriers that existed between them and the rest of society. Today had been his first attempt, and although it had not gone well, he promised himself he would not give up. Somehow there had to be a way not only to reach the poorest of the poor but also to help them out of their poverty.

Chapter 4

A Full-Time Preacher

"William, come here. I need to speak to you," Francis Eames said as he closed the ledger at the end of the day.

"Yes, sir," William replied. "What is it?"

Mr. Eames cleared his throat and adjusted his glasses. "I am sure you are aware that your apprenticeship will be up at the end of the month. I have decided not to keep you on as a journeyman. I'm sorry, but I am going to have to dismiss you and take on a new apprentice. It's much cheaper, and unpleasant decisions have to be made in these trying times. With your willingness to work hard and the way you get along with customers, I'm sure you will be able to find another job soon."

"Yes, sir," William said, wishing he could have thought of something more to add. But what could he say? He was about to lose his meager income and the roof over his head. And despite Francis Eames's optimism, he knew that getting another job would be difficult. Every day when he opened up the pawnshop there were big, strong men waiting outside to pawn the tools of their trade to get enough money for a loaf or two of bread. No employer that William knew was hiring men. Only women and children were being hired to work in the textile mills throughout the area.

A week later William packed his belongings and moved in with his mother and two younger sisters. There was a spare bed in one of the rooms over the shop because his older sister Ann had just married a hatter named Francis Brown and the newlyweds had moved to London in search of work.

Life for William soon fell into a frustrating routine. He was out of the house by eight o'clock in the morning, walking the grimy streets lined with red brick row houses. He stopped at every shop and business he came across asking if they would hire him, but nobody did. At lunchtime he returned home and helped his mother with some of the chores around her tiny shop. After that he headed out again for another round of fruitless job hunting. All day long William looked forward to his evening, when he would preach at a cottage meeting or in the streets. This was the work he really wanted to do, but no one he knew was willing to pay him to do it.

And the destitute of the city to whom he preached certainly did not have any spare cash to give him. Sundays William spent in church, preaching on the streets and studying the books and lecture notes of the great American preacher Charles Finney.

This routine continued on month after month. William tried not to eat too much of his mother's food, but even so he knew he was a drain on her resources and somehow, somewhere he needed to find a job.

After a year of fruitless searching, William had to admit that it was useless waiting for a job opening in Nottingham. He would have to move elsewhere. The obvious choice was London, since he could stay with his sister Ann. In February 1849, just before his twentieth birthday, William Booth boarded a train for Coventry with a connection on to London. It was hard saying good-bye to his mother, but William comforted himself with the knowledge that he would soon be able to send money back home to help support her and his two sisters.

William had never been on a train before, and he had never been more than a few miles from Nottingham. As the train journeyed south at thirty miles an hour, William watched as grimy industrial towns and lush green pastures rolled by. He thought about what he wanted to do in London. He knew two things: He needed to earn enough money to help his mother, and he did not want to work again as a pawnbroker. To him pawnbroking was soul-destroying work. Week after week he saw the same wretched people coming to pawn their clothes or tools on Wednesday to buy food or beer and then redeeming the items on Saturday, only to return with them again the following Wednesday. It was a horrible cycle to be a part of, and William was determined to find another way to earn his keep.

Finally the train pulled into London. William could scarcely believe the number of people jammed into the city. People were everywhere. Along with horses and carriages, they clogged the streets. Children in torn, dirty clothes begged for money from passersby while men and women alike crowded into the pubs that seemed to be located at every street corner.

Ann and Francis Brown lived only a couple of miles from the train station. After asking for directions, William set off to find their home. He was stunned when his sister opened the door and let him in.

"Why, William!" Ann exclaimed as she staggered toward him and flung her arms around his neck.

William sniffed the air. He knew the smell—alcohol. His sister was drunk!

"The house is a bit of a mess," Ann said as she scooped a half-empty bottle of liquor off the side table and stuffed it under a chair. "But sit down. I don't have any food at the moment, but it's my hope that Francis has sold a hat or two so that he can bring home bread and some suet for dinner."

As William sat listening to his sister ramble on, he could hardly believe it. She and Francis were living in a hovel with no food, and she was drunk before dinner. He had no idea what he was going to tell his mother in his first letter home.

It didn't take long for William to realize that both Francis and Ann spent most of their spare time drinking. They explained it away as a result of Francis's business not going well and Ann's being unable to find a job. William tried to help them understand that this was no way to live, but Francis grew increasingly angry at William's comments. Soon Ann told William that he would have to find somewhere else to live. But where could he go? He had not yet found a job.

Eventually William came to the unwelcome conclusion that he would have to go back to being a pawnbroker. It was the only job he was qualified for, and it always came with a room above the shop.

With a sad heart William said good-bye to his sister and moved into Filmer Pawnbroker's Shop in the suburb of Kennington, under the familiar symbol of three brass balls. The shop and his room were adequate enough. On the other side of the street from the store was a common, where rich young women paraded on Saturday afternoon while the young men played cricket.

Every night after work William would take his Bible and preach on the common or in the nearby streets. And just as in Nottingham, his Sundays were given over to attending church and running prayer meetings in the poorest areas of the city. Unlike his previous employer, however, Mr. Filmer had no tolerance for William's religious activities. He locked the doors at precisely 10 P.M. each evening, and if William was not inside by then, he had to sleep the night on the doorstep.

Soon William's enthusiasm for preaching was noticed by leaders in the Methodist church, and he was made an official lay preacher. This meant that he was now a recognized preacher within the church, though he received no pay for what he did. But the situation suited William. It was a step in a larger plan that was forming in his head.

After he had been in London for a year, William applied to become a full-time preacher. At the interview he confessed he was not interested in learning Latin grammar or Greek syntax. Instead he made an impassioned plea to be able to work among the very poorest people in London—the people who had never set foot in a church but who needed to hear that there was a way out of their grim daily existence.

It was a bitter day for William when he learned that the Methodist board had rejected his application on the grounds that he did not show enough interest in the intellectual aspects of Christianity. He poured out his frustration in a letter to a friend in Nottingham. He ended with the question, "How can anybody with spiritual eyesight talk of having no call when there are still multitudes around them who have never heard a word about God, and never intend to, who can never hear without the sort of preacher who can force himself upon them?"

William searched for other ways to become a full-time preacher. He considered applying to be a chaplain on a convict ship bound for Botany Bay in Australia, but he could not bear to desert his mother and younger sisters. He decided to keep working at the pawnshop and pray that God would open a way for him to give his full energies to reaching the lost with the gospel.

One Sunday in late March 1852, William preached at the Walworth Road Chapel. This was a new church that had sprung up because of a split between two groups within the Methodist church. William had never preached at Walworth Road Chapel before, but it turned out to be an event that would set him on a different path. In the congregation that day was a man named Edward Rabbits. Mr. Rabbits was legendary both inside and outside of Christian circles because he was a self-made man. Years before he had started a bootmaking enterprise with two and a half shillings of borrowed money. By the time he sat listening to William speak, he was a millionaire who owned a chain of shoe and bootmaking factories around London.

When William had finished his sermon, Edward Rabbits approached him. "Well done, lad!" he said enthusiastically. "Come to tea at my house today. There are certain matters I would like to discuss with you."

William walked slowly up Walworth Road to Mr. Rabbits's house. Part of him wished he had refused the invitation. He hated trying to make polite small talk with rich people. However, William soon found this was not what Edward Rabbits had in mind. No sooner had William removed his hat and coat than his host got straight to the point. "I have heard a lot about you, young man, and all of it is good. Tell me, how old are you?"

"Twenty-two years old," William replied, watching Mr. Rabbits's eyebrows rise.

"Well, you are young, younger than I thought; but still, you must leave the pawnbroking business and devote yourself wholly to preaching the gospel. You have a unique gift, and that gift should not be squandered on other things. Don't you agree?"

William was taken aback. Of course he agreed! But it wasn't as simple as that. "But," he stammered, "there is no way for me to do that. I have applied to the Methodists and been rejected. Nobody wants me."

"Nonsense!" bellowed Edward Rabbits. "You'll never get anywhere with an attitude like that. A man like you should be in full-time work."

William shook his head. "I cannot live on air. I have to work for my keep and to help support my widowed mother."

"How much do you need to live on?" Mr. Rabbits asked.

William thought for a moment. There was board, which cost at least five shillings a week, add another two shillings for food, and five more for transport and helping his mother out. "Twelve shillings," he announced. "I think I could get by on twelve shillings a week."

"Nonsense!" Edwards Rabbits said again. "No one can live decently on less than twenty shillings a week."

"Have it your way," William said. "It makes little difference to me because I have neither twelve nor twenty shillings a week to live on."

"But you *will* have," Mr. Rabbits said. "I believe you have a gift, and I want you to use it. Leave the pawnbroking business, and I will supply you with twenty shillings a week, for the first three months at least."

William hardly knew what to say. He had longed for a way to become a full-time preacher, and now that opportunity was being offered to him. It seemed an enormous step, but William was willing to try. "Thank you, Mr. Rabbits. I...I think I will avail myself of your kind offer."

"Good!" Edward Rabbits said, clapping him on the back. "What is to stop your giving notice to your employer tomorrow?"

"Nothing," William replied. "Absolutely nothing."

Chapter 5

An Extraordinary Person

Good Friday, April 10, 1852, was William Booth's twenty-third birthday. When he awoke that morning William was sure it was going to be a day he would never forget. It was the day he quit working for Filmer Pawnbroker's Shop and became a full-time preacher. As William packed his clothes and books into a bag, he had no idea there would be another important reason for him to remember the day.

William took one last look at the pawnshop and carried his belongings to Camberwell Street, where he had found cheap lodgings with a widow who made bonnets. The room he had rented was unfurnished, and William had already bought a bedstead and a table from the pawnshop to make it comfortable. Once he deposited his clothes and blankets in his new room, William decided to visit his sister Ann. He wanted to tell her the good news about his new position, even though he doubted she would be happy for him. Still, on a special day like Good Friday, William wanted to be with family.

William had just passed the end of City Road when he saw Edward Rabbits climbing out of a carriage. When Mr. Rabbits saw William, he called to him. "Ah, Mr. Booth, come. How are things with you?"

William crossed the street and took off his hat. "Fine, thank you, sir. In fact, things could not be better. Today is the first day of my freedom. I have left the pawnshop forever and embarked on my new life as a preacher."

"Glad to hear it!" Mr. Rabbits replied. "Come and see me on Monday morning, and I will arrange for you to draw the money off my account."

"Thank you, sir," William said. "I am eager to begin."

"Of course you are. Now, how about coming with me to Cooper Street School over there. We are having a tea meeting, and I would like to introduce you to some people who might be very useful to you one day."

William thought for a moment. He did want to see Ann, but this was too good an opportunity to miss. "I would be delighted," he said. "Lead the way."

Soon Edward Rabbits and William Booth were climbing the stone steps of the school. Inside a small group of Methodists were preparing a simple meal.

Mr. Rabbits guided William over to a petite woman with dark hair tied back into a bun, a dimple in her chin, and searching brown eyes. "William Booth," he said, "I would like you to meet a particular friend of mine, Miss Catherine Mumford."

Catherine smiled and offered William her hand. "Actually we have met before," she said. "About a year ago, I believe. We were engaged in a lively discussion on prohibition."

William scrambled to recall the occasion, but he could not. He had never paid much attention to the conversations he had with young women. "Oh," he replied vaguely. "And I hope we follow it up with another lively discussion tonight."

Suddenly William felt acutely self-conscious next to this well-dressed young woman. He wondered how he looked to her, with his mop of unruly black hair, beaked nose, and gaunt six-foot frame. He took small comfort in the fact that although his clothes were old and shapeless, at least they weren't patched!

Thankfully Catherine Mumford appeared to be able to overlook William's physical appearance, and the two of them spent much of the evening together talking. William learned that she was the only daughter of a coach builder and that she'd had four brothers. Three of them had died from various childhood illnesses, and the fourth, John, had emigrated to America when he was sixteen and had lost touch with her parents.

Catherine was a few months older than William, who changed the subject when she told him that she loved to read. He did not want to be quizzed on how many books he had read lately.

By the end of the evening, William noticed that Catherine was looking pale. "Are you ill?" he asked.

Catherine lowered her eyes. "I am feeling a little tired," she admitted. "I've had a problem with my back since I was a child, and sometimes sitting for long periods is difficult."

Just then Edward Rabbits interrupted the two of them. "Miss Mumford," he said, "I have taken the liberty of ordering a cab to take you home. Perhaps, Mr. Booth, you would accompany her and make sure she arrives safely."

William stood up. "Of course. I would be glad to do that. Come, Miss Mumford, let me get your coat for you."

William and Catherine talked all the way back to her home in Brixton. By the time they arrived at Catherine's door, William knew he was in the company of an extraordinary person. She was unlike any other woman he knew. She had opinions and knew how to argue them. She also had a firm conviction that men and women were equally capable of achieving great things.

Catherine's ideas both startled and impressed William. As he thought about them over the next few days, he found himself thinking more and more about marriage being a partnership between two equals—a partnership where two people could achieve more than either one could individually. As he thought about this, William came to the conclusion that he wanted Catherine Mumford to become his life's partner.

Falling in love, however, created a dilemma for William. He had met Catherine on the very day he had given up his profession and embarked upon a calling that paid him twenty shillings a week, and that was guaranteed for only three months. It was hardly the kind of credentials with which to court a young woman.

Still, William and Catherine were drawn to each other at a deep level, and despite William's lack of material prospects, they continued to see each other. A month later they were engaged, although no wedding date could be set until William had found a way to continue his preaching as well as support a wife.

Later in 1852 the opportunity to be recognized and supported by a church presented itself. The Reformed Methodists offered William the job of pastor of the Spalding circuit, a group of small churches in Lincolnshire, a hundred miles north of London. While it was a long way from London and Catherine, it was the best offer William had received now that Edward Rabbits was no longer financially supporting him. Mr. Rabbits had withdrawn his support of William over a theological disagreement.

William accepted the position, but as he traveled north to Lincolnshire, he was concerned about the new job. He was used to preaching in the open air.

How would he get on confining his messages to the same people sitting in the same pews week after week? As it happened, William need not have been concerned. From the start his preaching attracted new people to the services, and often eighteen or twenty new converts were added to the various churches in his circuit each week. Sometimes when a cottage meeting was announced, so many people would show up that the meeting had to be moved into the street outside. William was happiest of all when this happened.

Meanwhile Catherine wrote to him each day. Sometimes her letters were filled with practical advice about keeping his feet warm at all times and the benefits of eating raw eggs for breakfast. At other times she encouraged William to rise at 6 A.M. to study Greek and to preach on the usefulness of women in all areas of church life. She also wrote that some of her father's business deals had gone badly, leaving the family with little money, and that her neighbor had died in a cholera epidemic that had swept through London.

The more letters William received, the more he became convinced of two things. First, Catherine was an unusually strong and opinionated woman, and second, that is just what he needed in a life partner. The problem was that although he was a pastor in Spalding, William was not getting any closer to being able to marry Catherine. Although he made enough money for him to live on, his salary was hardly enough for a wife and the children who would inevitably follow. Besides, young circuit preachers were seldom given permission to marry by their overseers.

After eighteen months in Spalding, William was not sure what to do next. The answer came when he invited a guest evangelist, the Reverend Richard Poole, to ride his circuit with him. Listening to Richard Poole was eye-opening for William. The preacher was every bit as direct as William was, but his biblical scholarship came shining through as well. For the first time William saw his own need to study more, and so he wrote to Catherine explaining that he was coming back to London to study theology.

The theological college William chose to attend was associated with a group of Methodists who called themselves the New Connexion and was situated on Albany Road in South London. From the outset William found his studies difficult. His day started at 5 A.M., at least two hours earlier than he liked to get out of bed, and his days were filled with Greek and Latin study. Still, he was near Catherine, and with her help he managed to complete his study assignments.

It was William's passionate preaching that caught the attention of Dr. William Cooke, principal of the college. The first night William preached at the local Brunswick Chapel, fifteen people were converted, and it soon became widely known that if a chapel wanted a good, stirring service, it should invite William Booth to preach.

Soon William's reputation led Dr. Cooke to make William an unprecedented offer. He proposed that William become the superintendent of the New Connexion's London circuit. This was a huge step and one that William did not feel ready to take on, though he did agree to be the deputy superintendent. Dr. Cooke accepted the compromise and even offered to allow William to marry right away.

William and Catherine were of course overjoyed with this development, and they immediately set their wedding date for June 16, 1855. They had been engaged for almost three years. They were married in a small ceremony at Stockwell New Chapel, near William's school. William's mother and sister Mary could not afford to make the trip to London from Nottingham, but they pooled their money and sent his sister Emma along to represent the family. Sadly, his sister Ann and her husband were not there either. While William had been in Spalding, they had both died. William suspected they had drunk themselves to death.

The wedding was followed by William's first-ever vacation, a one-week honeymoon in Ryde, on the Isle of Wight. This was followed by a series of evangelistic preaching services on the nearby island of Guernsey. Much to William's alarm, Catherine became sick, and by the time they had returned to London, she had learned she was pregnant. Being too ill to travel any farther, she went to stay with her parents.

It was not an easy beginning to their marriage, but William had to go on with his work as deputy superintendent. Catherine encouraged him to also hold a series of revival meetings across England. She insisted that the pregnancy must not stand in the way of William's mission to preach.

So William set out alone, first to Lincoln, then Bristol, Manchester, and Sheffield, preaching in New Connexion chapels. Along the way he developed a system for dealing with the many people who were converted by his preaching. He invited those who were interested in becoming Christians to the communion rail at the front of the church. William always made sure that two church deacons were waiting there to escort them into a side room. There the new converts were asked their names and addresses and paired up with someone in the congregation who promised to make sure the new convert got a Bible and came to church regularly. All of this follow-up was new and revolutionary, but William felt it was essential. What was the use, he argued, of saving a soul unless one also made sure it was nurtured and fed?

William longed to return to London to be with his wife, but he knew she would not want him to do that. Catherine had insisted from the day they met that he put his work for God first.

As the date of the baby's arrival approached, William returned to London by train. On March 8, 1856, Catherine gave birth to a son. They named him William Bramwell, after an evangelist who had preached his way through northern England fifty years before. Bramwell Booth, who had his mother's dimple and his father's long legs, was a strong, healthy child from the start. The following year, on July 28, 1857, Catherine gave birth to a second son, whom they named Ballington after Catherine's favorite great uncle. During this time the growing Booth family had no home of their own, and they stayed with friends or in make-shift rented rooms.

Finally, two years after he and Catherine were married, William completed his preaching tour of Great Britain, and the family settled into a house together. They did so just in time, because baby number three was born on September 18, 1858. This time it was a girl, whom they christened Catherine.

From London, the New Connexion assigned William to a church in a small mill town in Yorkshire called Brighouse and then to Gateshead, a stone's throw from the huge industrial city of Newcastle. In Gateshead, on January 8, 1860, William and Catherine's fourth child, a daughter named Emma, was born.

William had plenty to do inside the church, but it was the people outside, the people who never dreamed of setting a foot inside a church, who really concerned him. As he looked out his study window, William would ask himself, *In how many of those gray, dreary homes is the name of Christ ever mentioned? What am I doing here in a chapel filled with Christians who are eager to learn about God when I could be out there bringing the message to those who do not want to hear it?*

Despite his desire to be ministering to those who never set foot in church, William did his best to be a good pastor. Two years passed, until something happened inside the church that stirred up everyone, including William.

Chapter 6

Catherine's Preaching Gift

It was Whitsunday 1860, and William stood at the pulpit preaching. Looking out at the congregation, he saw Catherine, with four-year-old Bramwell sitting beside her, and several local dignitaries who had come to hear him. Just as he was about to announce the final hymn, William noticed Catherine stand up and walk deliberately down the aisle and up the altar steps. His mind raced. What could possibly be important enough for her to interrupt the service? Perhaps there was a disturbance outside or she was feeling ill.

As his wife's skirt swished up to him, William whispered, "What is it, my dear?"

She looked at him with steady eyes. "I want to say a word."

"At the pulpit?" he whispered back.

Catherine nodded.

William was astonished. Women did not take over the pulpit! But he knew that Catherine must have some good reason to do such a strange thing, so he turned to the congregation. "My dear wife wishes to speak," he said and then sat down.

Catherine spoke in a clear, high voice. "I dare say many of you have been looking at me as a very devoted woman, but I have disobeyed God. I have made a promise to God that I will obey Him from now on, and it was His Holy Spirit who urged me to stand up and speak to you all. I, like my husband, have been called to preach the gospel from the pulpit, and I am ready to do that, even if it means that I look like a fool—at least I shall be a fool for Christ."

William looked out over the congregation. Many people were weeping. Catherine continued to talk for a few more minutes, and then she beckoned William to step up to the pulpit. William hurried to her and whispered in her ear, "I can see that God is moving through your words. Will you preach again tonight?"

Catherine nodded, and William stepped forward to the pulpit. "My dear wife will be the preacher tonight," he announced.

Following Whitsunday many people questioned William as to why he had allowed a woman to take over his pulpit. He always gave the same answer: His goal was to bring curious people within the sound of the gospel, and if a woman preacher, or anyone else for that matter, helped to do that, William was all for it.

As it happened, soon afterward Catherine was able to put her newfound preaching skills to work helping William through a difficult time. When William collapsed from nervous stress, she took over his preaching and visiting duties at church until he recovered. And once William recovered, he and Catherine together formed a determined team.

Of course, not everyone was happy about this. A woman preacher was outside the comprehension of most Methodists. Christian wives were supposed to be at home looking after the children or sewing kneeling cushions, not standing up in front of men telling them how to live their lives! Complaints, along with some compliments, began to pour into the New Connexion headquarters. By May 1861, the date of the annual conference, the future of the preaching team of William and Catherine Booth had become a contentious issue. William had asked the conference to release him from his church responsibilities so that he and Catherine could run revival meetings in New Connexion churches throughout the area.

On Saturday, May 25, the matter finally came to a head. Dr. Cooke, principal of William's old seminary, stepped in with a suggestion that he hoped would address the concerns of many while opening the door for William and Catherine to hold their revival meetings.

"How would it be," Dr. Cooke asked the conference, "if William Booth was put in charge of the entire Newcastle circuit. Then, when things were going smoothly, he could take time off to hold revival meetings in other areas."

William's heart sank. This was not what he had been hoping for. For one thing, no mention was made of Catherine's preaching gift, and for another, he doubted if things would ever be running smoothly enough in Newcastle for him to "take time off." Newcastle was a very difficult area to be the superintendent of.

A discontented murmur went through the crowd at Dr. Cooke's suggestion. The president of the New Connexion, Dr. Crofts, stepped to the front and glared at those in the room.

"This will not do!" Dr. Crofts boomed. "We must have order. Clear the public gallery, and we will continue to discuss William Booth's future in a closed session."

There was a scurry of activity behind him, and then William heard a strong, clear voice rise from the gallery. "No…never!" It was Catherine. William looked around to see his wife being escorted toward the door. At that moment William Booth made a choice. His fate would not be discussed in secret away from his wife and the members of his congregation who had come to support him. William stood up, waved his hat in the air as a salute to his wife, and walked deliberately out the door. Catherine was standing on the steps, and he hooked her arm in his and headed down the street. Neither of them looked back. William's days of being a New Connexion pastor were over.

The question William now had to grapple with was, what lay ahead? He was a thirty-two-year-old man with a wife and four small children to house and feed. After mulling over the problem for two months, William still had no answer as to what to do next. The family had just enough money to buy train tickets and return to London. Should they go there, or should they stay and buy food? William and Catherine prayed hard about the situation and in the end came to the conclusion that they should return to London to live with Catherine's parents while they waited to see what doors of ministry would open up for them. They packed their bags and set off for London.

As soon as they were settled into the Mumfords' home, William began looking for work. He got the occasional odd job and spent the money he earned on soup bones and two-day-old bread to feed the family. Yet he never doubted that he had done the right thing in resigning from the New Connexion. He knew his future lay in preaching. He just wished the situation were not so hard on Catherine and the children. When he tried to apologize to his wife for the way things had worked out, Catherine replied, "Trust in God, William. He will not give us more than we are able to bear. A way will open for us soon. You will see."

And a way did open up, though for William not a very promising one. John Stone, a convert from William's Chester revival meetings, had become a pastor in Hayle, Cornwall. The Reverend Stone wrote a letter inviting William and Catherine to preach in his chapel, though he warned that his congregation was small and elderly and that the chapel could afford to offer him only a few shillings' remuneration for his efforts. It was the only offer William had, and he gladly accepted. In August 1861 the Booths left their children with the Mumfords and traveled to Cornwall.

Since he had last seen John Stone, William had been experimenting with a new format for his revival meetings. This new format involved inviting members of the audience who wanted to repent of their sins and become Christians to come to the front of the church. There they publicly stood at the "penitent rail," confessed their sins, and asked Jesus to come into their lives. The New Connexion leaders had opposed this way of doing things because they felt it made too much of a show over sin, that it was better for such matters to be dealt with in a private manner. Thankfully, the Reverend Stone agreed with William's approach and gave him permission to use a penitent rail in the chapel.

The results of the meetings in Hayle were astounding, even to William and Catherine. Each day the number of people attending the special services grew, until fishermen were rowing ten miles across rough seas to reach the chapel, while others, including families with young children, hiked over the coastal trails to get there. At every meeting a mixture of people from burly miners to little old ladies to young people stood together at the front of the chapel, weeping and asking God to forgive them for their sins.

News of what was happening in Hayle spread throughout the neighboring towns, and soon William and Catherine were invited to speak in churches all over Cornwall. In the nearby town of St. Just, more than a thousand people joined local churches in the time the Booths spent there. And in St. Ives so many people came to the meetings that the newspaper reported the town was all but shut down. All of the shopkeepers and customers were involved in the revival meetings.

Other eyes were watching the Booths as well. The Methodists were pleased to see their churches and funds growing. The *Wesleyan Times* reported:

> During the eighteen weeks Mr and Mrs Booth conducted their services in Redruth and Camborne at least 3,000 souls were brought to Jesus.... At Redruth we hear the Free Church has given 1,500 pounds for ground and we are going to build immediately the largest chapel in the country.... Since Mr and Mrs Booth commenced their evangelistic work in Cornwall 7,000 souls have been awakened and saved.

Although these leaders liked the growing churches and funds, they were not particularly impressed with a wayward pastor stirring up so much emotion in the people. They argued that revival was "unseemly" and "undignified" and had to be stopped. So the leaders of the Methodist church ordered the pastors of their churches to close their doors and pulpits to the Booths. William and Catherine were shocked by the decision, as were many local pastors. Soon other denominations began following the example of the Methodists in barring the Booths.

William and Catherine returned to London saddened by the knowledge that despite seven thousand people being converted under their preaching, they were no longer welcome in most churches. But having tasted success in their preaching, neither William nor Catherine was ready to give up holding revival meetings.

Back in London, on August 26, 1862, Catherine gave birth to another son, whom they named Herbert. Even with five children, Catherine urged William to find a way for them to continue their preaching work. The question was, how?

William decided that he and Catherine would continue their preaching with or without the backing of the Methodists, or anyone else for that matter. In January 1863 they left the children once again in the care of Catherine's mother and went to Wales. As expected, the doors to all the major churches were closed to them. Instead of holding the revival meetings in churches, William hired a circus tent for the purpose and advertised the gathering. Many people came, including drunks, pickpockets, and bookies.

William immediately saw the advantage of holding such meetings outside of established churches. "Godless surroundings attract godless people," he told Catherine joyfully.

During these meetings William also discovered that although the people in the tent listened to him as he preached, they paid rapt attention when one of their own stood and told the audience his or her story. A former drunk testified how he had found peace for the first time in his life. As a result he had gone home and poured a barrel of beer out on the street. His neighbors had asked what he was doing, and he told them. Now half of those who lived on his street were seated in the meeting. Time after time, poachers, horse racers, and wife beaters stood up to tell how God had changed their hearts and their behavior.

All of this confirmed to William that he was on the right path. For the next two years, he and Catherine preached at all sorts of venues around England and Wales. Two Welsh brothers, John and Richard Cory, who had become rich from coal mining and shipping ventures, offered to help with the Booths' living expenses. William and Catherine sent for their children, and together the family lived the life of itinerant preachers. In the spring of 1864 Catherine gave birth to a sixth baby, a girl whom they named Marian.

William found himself back in London in July 1865. The family had taken up temporary residence in the suburb of Hammersmith. On Sunday afternoon, July 2, William set out from the house for the eight-mile walk to Mile End Road in London's East End. As he walked, he was shocked by what he saw. The city was in an even worse state than he had remembered. As he approached the East End, the row houses were dirty and dilapidated. Often as many as forty or fifty people were living in one house. They had little or no running water and used the gutter as a bathroom. And every fifth store in the area was a gin shop serving rot-gut liquor to anyone who could pay. These shops had special steps at the bar so that children, many younger than five years old, could step up and buy penny glasses of gin. It was not uncommon to see these children passed out on the street or suffering the effects of delirium tremens (DTs), a sure sign of alcoholism. Their tiny livers were much more affected by alcohol than those of the adults who callously introduced it to them. Such scenes both shocked and saddened William, who longed to do something to help the people trapped in these deplorable conditions.

William's destination that day was an abandoned Quaker burial ground in Whitechapel, where he had been hired by the East End Revival Society to hold a series of tent meetings. As he picked his way around the broken pavement and heaps of garbage, he imagined he would be holding revival meetings there for six weeks before moving on to another town or city. William had no idea as he walked along that he was about to step into his destiny.

Chapter 7

A Lifetime's Worth of Work

I am glad to meet you, Mr. Booth," said a Quaker man who was waiting outside the tent. "My name is Charles York, and I have everything ready for you. Come and see. I'm sorry, but I'll be out of town from tomorrow on, so you will have to find someone to help you set up the benches for the meetings or do it yourself."

William stepped inside the old circus tent. Its sides were worn thin enough to see daylight through them, and several of the corners had been ripped and repaired. Rows of wooden benches were set out on the bare ground.

"This will do fine!" William said.

"I certainly hope so," Charles York replied. He then dropped his voice low before continuing. "Our

Quaker meeting voted to allow this burial ground to be used for a year. So far the tent has been up for six months. Various preachers have come and gone, but they have made little impact on the people who live around here. There are over a million of them, poor souls, who live within a mile of this tent—and nine out of ten of them have never once heard the gospel." He shook his head for emphasis as he spoke.

William stood in silence for a moment, looking at the tent. It probably seated two hundred people at most, but there were over a million people less than a five-minute walk from where he was standing! Excitement surged through him. This was the kind of challenge he was looking for—the kind of challenge he could give his life to.

William prepared for the first service as best he could. He talked a young lamplighter into helping him string the naphtha lights in the tent and lashed the flaps down.

For William all the preparation work was worth it, and when he stood to speak early that evening, people trickled in to hear what he had to say. A young girl carried a basket of wilting flowers she was trying to sell, an older woman sat near the back darning a pair of socks, and a group of dirty-faced boys sat sheepishly near the front.

Soon William launched into a simple sermon. "Imagine a man going down a river in a boat," he began. "He is headed for the Niagara Falls, but he does not know what is ahead of him, nor does he care. The weather is nice, the sun is shining, and he's not worried about a thing. He paddles out into the stream, and suddenly he feels the current tugging him. He is going, going…"

William paused for dramatic effect and leaned over as if he were peering down a cavernous hole. "My God!" he yelled. "The boater has gone over—and he never pulled at an oar! That is the way people are damned: They go on, they have no time, they don't think—they neglect salvation—and they are lost!"

From there William went on to explain how Jesus offers salvation to anyone who asks for it. By the time the sermon was over, the tent was half full, and six people were standing at the penitent rail, ready to give their lives to God. One of these six people was a quiet man who introduced himself as James Flawn. He fidgeted with his cap as he talked to William.

"I own a small tearoom at Pudding Lane," James began, "and I want to help. I'm not much good at talking or the like, but I know how to arrange chairs. If you're needing someone, I'd be willing to straighten up the benches before and after each meeting, sir."

William thanked him for his offer and then spent over an hour with the new converts, explaining to them the basic principles of Christian living. Before setting out on the eight-mile walk home, he told them that he hoped they would return for the following day's meeting.

William burst into the house and swept Catherine into a hug. "I have found my destiny!" he shouted. "I have found a place where there is so much human misery in such a small space that there is a lifetime's worth of work there for me! Why go farther afield for audiences when they lie at our doorstep? Oh, Catherine, this takes me back to the days when I was an apprentice by day and a preacher by night. Now I see I was never meant to preach inside a church. Where's the challenge in that? It's only in keeping the congregation awake. But the people I preached to today were awake. True, they were fidgeting, heckling, spitting, and arguing—but they were awake!"

Catherine laughed. "I have seldom seen you so excited, William! I have something to tell you as well."

William drew quiet immediately. "What is it, my dear?"

"Today the trustees at the Eyre Arms Assembly asked me to conduct a series of meetings for them."

"How wonderful!" William replied. "God is using both of us in London, though our congregations are as different as I can imagine."

Catherine nodded in agreement. "I am sure that this will open the door for me to preach to some of the wealthiest men in London while you are laboring in the slums. Let's trust that God is in both works."

"And what about your health?" William questioned. "Won't your back get sore standing for that long?"

Catherine smiled. "My back hurts whether I stand or not, and besides, the baby's not due until Christmas. I can't put my life on hold until then. There is so much to do. Thank goodness we have a nanny now, and I'm sure my mother will help out when the time comes. Though I'm not sure about little Marian. The doctor says she's made a full recovery from the smallpox, but she doesn't seem the same as she did before she got ill. Somehow she doesn't seem as alert as before," Catherine concluded as she pulled a wisp of hair back into her bun. "We must trust God and go on."

William nodded. "We've come this far, and with God's help we shall trust Him with our future." Then he could not resist getting back to the topic of the tent meeting. "You should have seen it! So many opportunities, I hardly know where to begin!"

Over the next few weeks William came home at all hours of the night with wonderful stories to tell Catherine. There was the conversion of "Mother" Moore, a Whitechapel charwoman who was hardly ever sober. She came to a meeting and swore she would never drink again. When her old drinking companions offered her alcohol, she would chide them, "I can drink from the wells of salvation—and so can you!" After her conversion Mother Moore came to every one of William's meetings, where she often helped James Flawn set out the benches and stack them away afterward.

There was opposition to William's preaching, but William thrived on action and did everything he could to draw attention to his meetings. Sometimes, when the crowd was small, he would gather his converts and march down to a pub. They would stand outside and sing hymns until the drinkers came out to see what the commotion was. They would then invite everyone to march back to the tent with them to hear William preach. This often worked, and it wasn't long before the pub owners despised William. They paid young boys to slash the tent and throw rotten fruit and garbage at him. None of this bothered William, even when he was pushed and shoved to the ground. He merely stood up again and continued preaching where he had left off.

One of the early converts at William's East End revival meetings was Peter Monk, a brawny Irish boxer. Now that he was a Christian, he did not want to fight anymore, and seeing the way William was being treated, he appointed himself William's personal bodyguard. He walked with William the eight miles to and from the East End each day. During the services he sat watchfully in the front row. If any of the local gangs of boys burst into the meeting intent on making trouble, they soon found themselves in Peter Monk's strong grip.

July turned into August, and August into September. Regrettably, the tent had been slashed and mended so many times that it was useless for keeping out the autumn cold. However, since William was more convinced than ever that this area of the city was where he belonged, he persuaded the East London Christian Mission to rent a building for him to preach in instead of the tent. Not many buildings were available to choose from, and at first they could hire a building to hold only Sunday services in. The building was a dance hall on New Road, in Whitechapel. At four o'clock on Sunday mornings, William, Bramwell, and a small band of converts arrived at the dance hall to clean up after the Saturday night dance and set out three hundred chairs for the morning service. At the end of the day, after the service was over, they had to stack away the chairs.

November saw another move for the Booth family. Catherine found a house for rent in Hackney, which was not far from the East End. The family, along with their Irish nanny, Mary Kirkton, moved into Number 1 Cambridge Lodge Villa.

After the family moved into the new house, the older boys began attending the local school, though they did not have an easy time of it. Bramwell found it especially difficult to fit in. He was a tall, shy boy who was partially deaf. Soon after starting school, he came home one day bloody from head to toe. As he staggered in the door, William rushed to help him to a chair. "What happened?" he asked in a loud voice so that Bramwell could hear.

Tears danced in Bramwell's eyes as he looked at his father. "After school some of the boys called me a Holy Roller, and when I didn't reply, they picked me up and banged my head against a tree in the school yard. I lost count after they had done it eight times."

William reached out and put his arms around his oldest son. "We must all be prepared to suffer for Christ's sake," he told him. "One day you will see that it is an honor."

That night, after Bramwell was washed and bandaged, William and Catherine sat in the parlor for a long time. "There is no doubt the children are having an unusual upbringing," Catherine said, "and I suppose we can only expect they will bear some of the burden for our calling. After all, you come home with cuts and bruises many nights yourself, and I am billed as the 'Amazing Female Preacher.' As much as it pains me to see them suffer, God has called us to follow Him, and that does not stop just because we have six children."

William agreed. Anyone who spent an hour in their home had time enough to observe that every aspect of their lives was related to their Christian beliefs. William smiled as he thought about the burned-out hollow in the nursery table—the result of repeated "burnt offerings" the children enacted as a way to dispose of their broken Noah's ark animals. When their nanny was not watching, they lit a fire in the center of the table and ceremoniously burnt any animals that were broken beyond repair. And there was the time William crept into the nursery to see Ballington playing at being the preacher. Ballington's sisters Catherine, whom everyone called Kate, and Emma were the congregation. Each girl held two dolls and pretended they were crying and fussing. Ballington turned to them and commanded, "Take those babies out of the theatre."

At that point, Kate said with smug satisfaction, "Papa would not have stopped—he would have gone on preaching and let the babies cry!"

William retreated, chuckling to himself. Neither he nor Catherine lectured the children about religious matters, but each child was working out his or her own role in a family of preachers.

William encouraged everyone who was converted through his preaching to go to a nearby church. There were plenty to pick from—St. Paul's Cathedral, Westminster Abbey, or All Hallows—but the inhabitants of the slum would not go to any of them. Some complained, "The likes of us are not welcome there," or "We stood at the door, but the deacon told us to go around to the back and sit on the vestry steps, where we could listen to the sermon." Others offered excuses: "Me sisters and me don't have a Sunday dress between us, and our pa's never had a collar on in his life."

This concerned William. He knew that the people were telling the truth. After all, he had not forgotten what had happened years before when he had tried and failed to introduce poor people to his own congregation back in Nottingham. But if those who attended his revival meetings would not go to an existing church, what would become of them? Who would help them read the Bible and grow in their new Christian lives?

William had no answer to these questions as more and more converts kept coming back to the revival meetings instead of attending established churches. In fact, so many people were coming that by November 1865 the dance hall was too small. William hired a warehouse on Three Colts Lane in which to hold his meetings. This was a huge building with high windows and no insulation. Inside it was freezing cold in winter and stifling hot in summer. One of the causes of the heat in summer was having to leave the windows shut. This was because of the steady stream of projectiles that were hurled into the meetings from the outside, mostly by unruly boys. On one occasion, seeking to disrupt a meeting in progress, several boys set a match to a trail of gunpowder. The flare from the powder set the dress of one of the women in the audience aflame. People rushed to her aid and beat out the flames. Despite these attempts to disrupt his meetings, William Booth remained resolute. He used the story of the woman with her dress on fire as an illustration for a sermon, and through it all he kept preaching.

As December rolled around, everyone waited for the arrival of the newest Booth baby. William was delighted when Evangeline was born on December 25, 1865. He joined Catherine in a prayer for their new baby daughter, and then he wrapped the baby in a blanket and carried her out to show the other children. They were in the middle of breakfast, though three-year-old Herbert had climbed down from his chair and was peering with awe at the snowy scene outside. "Come and look," William said tenderly to the children. "Here is God's Christmas gift to us."

"Is it a girl or a boy?" Ballington asked.

"It's a girl," William replied, "and we are going to call her Evangeline, or Eva for short."

"After the Eva in *Uncle Tom's Cabin*?" Bramwell inquired.

"That's right. I can't think of a better name than that, can you?" William said.

Everyone took a turn holding the new baby, and then William carried her back to Catherine.

Baby Eva thrived from the beginning, and soon the older children were carrying her to William's meetings. Sadly, by this time it was obvious that eighteen-month-old Marian had been permanently damaged by her earlier bout with smallpox. She suffered from fits and was not as mentally alert as the older children had been at the same age.

William now had sixty loyal followers who helped him run the revival meetings and counsel and encourage the growing number of converts in their new faith. Most of these loyal followers were from the ranks of the poorest Londoners, but several were men and women of influence. One such man was a young medical student at London Hospital named Thomas Barnardo. During 1865 he had often helped William with his indoor meetings, but as 1866 dawned, he told William he was leaving to open a home for homeless boys in Stepney.

William looked into the determined eyes of the young man and said, "You look after the children, and I'll look after the adults." He clapped Thomas on the shoulder and added, "Then together we'll convert the world."

William meant what he said. Although he now had sixty loyal followers helping him and people were coming forward at every meeting to become Christians, William still had a long, long way to go to reach his goal.

Chapter 8

A Growing Work

William chuckled as he opened the *East London Observer* and spread the newspaper out on the table. "Come and look at this, Catherine!"

"What is it, William?" his wife asked, carrying Lucy, the latest addition to the Booth family. Lucy had been born just months before, on April 28, 1868.

"It's about my work," William said. He read the article aloud:

> This gentleman has for some time past occupied the Effingham Theatre on Sunday evenings as a preaching place, and enormous audiences have been drawn to listen to his exordiums by the somewhat plagiaristic announcements of "Change of Performance"

> and "Wanted! 3,000 men to fill the Effingham Theatre. The Rev. William Booth will preach in this theatre on Sunday evening next!"
>
> The result of so novel a promise as a change of performance, coupled with a formidable body of people marching down Whitechapel Road singing, we are bound to say with not the most melodious of harmonies, no doubt drew many persons who might even now be ignorant of the exact kind of "performance" so vaguely shadowed forth by the bills. The boxes and stalls were filled with as idle and dissolute a set of characters as ever crossed a place of public resort.

"That's not very complimentary, is it?" Catherine said.

"Probably not! But what does it matter?" William replied. "It's all free publicity. I don't care what they say about me as long as they say something—and announce where I'm preaching."

"I suppose you're right," Catherine said, and then with a chuckle she added, "and some of those billboards you use are eye-catching. Didn't I see Bramwell wearing a sandwich board last Sunday that read, 'Come drunk or sober'?"

"It was his idea," William retorted in mock indignation. "Kate had one that read 'Come Early to Get a Seat!' And that was her idea too. I think we are finally starting to make a mark—a small one, mind you, but a mark." He looked at the newspaper once again; "'...filled with as idle and dissolute a set of characters as ever crossed a place of public resort.' Those are just the people I am trying to reach—the more idle and dissolute the better. None of the churches are reaching out to these lost souls. They are my people, Catherine, my people."

A week later a more favorable article appeared in the *Nonconformist.* William read it aloud to Catherine:

> The labouring people and the roughs have it [the theatre]—much to their satisfaction—all to themselves. It is astonishing how quiet they are.
>
> There is no one except a stray official to maintain order; yet there are nearly two thousand persons belonging to the lowest and least educated classes behaving in a manner which would reflect the highest credit upon the most respectable congregation that ever attended a regular place of worship....
>
> Mr. Booth employed very simple language in his comments...frequently repeated the same sentence several times as if he was afraid his hearers would forget. It was curious to note the intense, almost painful degree of eagerness with which every sentence of the speaker was listened to. The crowd seemed fearful of losing even a word....
>
> There was no sign of impatience during the sermon. There was too much dramatic action, too much anecdotal matter to admit

> of its being considered dull, and when it terminated scarcely a person left his seat, indeed some appeared to consider it too short, although the discourse had occupied fully an hour in its delivery.

"This is our year, Catherine, I know it," William said. "We are on the move!"

And so they were. By the end of 1868, the East London Christian Mission, the organization William had formed, now had thirteen "preaching stations" (though he had to admit that some of them were nothing more than a permanent presence on a street corner). Some of the newest stations included the Oriental Theatre on Poplar High Street, a large shop on Hackney Road, and the New East London Theatre in Whitechapel. Various mission preachers held 140 revival meetings a week. Altogether there were seats for eight thousand people at these services. And since many of the venues held more than one meeting a week, William estimated that over fourteen thousand people were coming through the doors—or tent flaps—of the East London Christian Mission every week.

By now the revival meetings had branched out to include many other activities that William saw as essential to getting men and women out of abject poverty. These activities included evening classes in reading and writing, mothers' meetings, religious tract discussion groups, temperance rallies, and soup kitchens. William intended to reach the whole person and help pull him or her up from whatever depths the person had sunk to.

William even launched a lively sixteen-page monthly newsletter to inform people about everything that was going on. He called it the *East London Evangelist,* and it carried eye-catching headlines, including "A Raging Mob Defied" and "Lob Those Rotten Apples!"

At the end of a busy year, William and Catherine decided it was time for the family to move yet again. A new church was being built beside their existing house, and Catherine found the constant banging of hammers and yelling of the workmen unbearable. The Booths' new address was Belgrave House, Number 3 Gore Road, Hackney. The three-story house was surrounded by a brick wall with iron railings, and across the road was Victoria Park. To help pay the rent on the place, the Booths took in two women lodgers.

Christmas Day 1868 was upon them soon after the move to the new house. William preached in the morning, but he knew the children were waiting eagerly at home to open their presents. However, by the time he had walked home through the grim streets of East London, his own Christmas spirit had evaporated. He went inside and sat silently by the fire.

"Papa, Papa. Come and play the fox and geese with us," said Eva, who was also celebrating her third birthday.

In this game William was the fox and the children the geese. He would chase them around the house until he caught each one. It was the family's favorite indoor game.

"Soon," he said, tousling Eva's hair.

After his daughter left the room, William began pacing across the hearth rug. Half an hour later Catherine came in rocking Lucy in her arms. "What is it, William?" she asked.

William paced back and forth two more times and then sat in the leather armchair by the fire. Catherine sat down opposite him. Waterford, the family's faithful retriever, plopped himself down at William's feet.

"It was so depressing walking home today," William began. "I know I see the same sights every day, but today should be different—it's Christmas. But still the streets are filled with drunk, wretched children and adults. It's Christ's birthday, and they have nothing to look forward to. Look at Lucy. We have this big house and food, and she has a family that loves her and cares for her. Her future is filled with hope, but those people out there on the streets—they have no hope. They are dirty and ragged and lost. We must do something about it. I'll never again spend a Christmas like this."

"What do you have in mind?" Catherine asked soothingly.

"It's not much, but it will be a start. Next Christmas why don't we make Christmas puddings and distribute them in the slums? We have to find a way to bring some hope to people on Christmas," William replied.

A week later, on the afternoon of New Year's Eve, William was preparing his sermon for the evening service. The title was "What Are You Going to Do in 1869?" He was putting the finishing touches to it when the doorbell rang. Soon afterward Emma brought in a telegram. William looked at the sender's address. The telegram was from Henry Reed, a rich Methodist man who lived some distance away in Tunbridge Wells. In the telegram Henry Reed asked William to visit him as soon as possible, by means of that evening's train if he could. William had no idea why he was being summoned at such short notice, but he handed the sermon he was preparing to Catherine for her to deliver and headed for the train.

Henry Reed was waiting at the train station in Tunbridge Wells to meet William. "Mr. Booth, so good of you to come," he said, holding out his hand to shake William's.

The two men rode in a carriage to Henry Reed's estate. The house was expansive and exquisitely decorated. Fine Persian rugs adorned the floors, and the furniture was made of mahogany imported from Asia. A servant took William's coat as he stepped inside, and then Henry guided William to the drawing room, where a large fire blazed in the hearth. William made himself comfortable on a sofa beside a well-stocked bookshelf, and Henry sat in a wing-backed chair opposite him.

After a maid had brought in a pot of tea and served a cup to each man, the two men got down to serious conversation.

"No doubt you are wondering why I asked you to come," Henry began.

William nodded.

"My concern is with the financial well-being of your mission, Mr. Booth. I have taken an option on a piece of land in the East End, near where your original tent meetings were held. I am willing to build a meeting hall on this land for you to hold your meetings in. You may review the plans and make any alterations you desire. When it is finished, the building will be entirely at your disposal."

"That is a very kind offer, sir," William said, a little startled but feeling very relieved. Perhaps 1869 was going to be the year he could finally stop worrying about the family's bills!

Henry cleared his throat. "There are, however, a few minor conditions attached with this offer."

"Go on," William replied, leaning forward in his seat.

"First, you will hold no more Sunday services in hired theatres. Paying rent for these places on Sunday as you do only helps finance the godless activities that go on in them the rest of the week. Second, you must agree to fill this new hall each time you hold meetings there. If you agree to these conditions and abide by them, I will financially support your ministry. However, if you fail to live up to them, I shall have no other option but to withdraw my support and reclaim the deed to the new building and the land on which it will sit. What do you say? That doesn't sound too difficult for you, does it?"

William sat quietly for a few moments mulling over Henry Reed's offer. It was an attractive one, one that would guarantee William personally some measure of financial stability and provide a permanent facility in which to carry out his ministry. There would be no more lugging chairs in and out of dance halls, no more setting up tents on vacant lots, no more chilling winds sweeping through broken windows of old factories, no more competing against the squeals of pigs being slaughtered in the market area. But no matter how attractive the offer was, William knew he could not accept it. In doing so he would be serving Henry Reed and his conditions and not God. William knew that he had to be free to follow God's leading. "I thank you for your kind offer, sir," William said, "but I am afraid I cannot accept it."

After spending the night at Henry Reed's home, William returned to London the following morning, New Year's Day 1869. He did not have a doubt that he had done the right thing in turning down the offer. The words of the sermon he had been preparing the day before came back to him as a personal challenge: "What are you going to do in 1869?" William realized that the great test of character is *doing*. God, the church, and society at large all estimate a man not according to his sayings, feelings, or desires but according to the things he does. William knew he needed to be free to do whatever God showed him to do, without caring what Henry Reed or anyone else would say.

Even without Henry Reed's help, the East London Christian Mission continued to grow at a fast clip during 1869. Mission workers fanned out to the worst areas of the city. It was impossible to enter a pub without first being offered a pamphlet by a worker or to leave one without an invitation to a soup kitchen or Christian tearoom.

Even the British Parliament was taking notice, and some of its members began sending money to William to help in his fight against poverty.

The rapid growth of the ministry was mostly due to the way in which new converts were encouraged to take a full part in the services and activities offered. William believed that they could be effective Christian workers from the time they were converted. Certainly they had many rough edges, but he would point out time and time again that those rough edges were what enabled them to relate to others who were trapped in the endless cycles of poverty and drink.

In April 1869 a group of young women from the mission got together and announced they were forming themselves into the Christian Female Pioneers. On William's fortieth birthday the women told him they wanted to start a cottage prayer meeting and a night school for children in the infamous London suburb of Bethnal Green.

William knew that most Christian leaders would insist that men accompany any group of women workers to such a dangerous place, and even direct their work, but he had been married to Catherine too long to stand in the way of determined women! He had come to believe that women and men were completely equal in God's sight and were capable of doing the same things. His two oldest daughters, ten-year-old Kate and nine-year-old Emma, were also starting to be a help to the mission. They would go out onto the streets to gather groups of poor children to preach to, and they often spoke at cottage meetings.

The Christian Female Pioneers were an instant success, or at least in the way William defined success. His favorite verse of cheer was Matthew chapter 5 verse 12: "Blessed are ye when men shall revile you and persecute you and say all manner of evil against you falsely for my sake." The women were taunted and pelted with rotten fruit by the residents of Bethnal Green for their efforts, but they would not give up, and soon a cottage meeting sprang up in the area.

In August William traveled to Edinburgh, where a group called the Edinburgh Friends ran a mission similar to the East London Christian Mission, only on a much smaller scale. The Edinburgh Friends approached William and asked if they could become part of his mission. William agreed enthusiastically. The East London Christian Mission was beginning to spread its wings.

While the mission was rapidly growing, William was determined not to lose sight of the simple message of salvation and offering a helping hand to the poor. At Christmas that year he made good on his pledge to bring cheer to the slums. The entire Booth family labored together to mix up 150 puddings and boil them at home in the family's laundry copper. Their new kitchen helper Polly joined in too. On Christmas morning everyone helped deliver the puddings.

Over the next three years, the East London Christian Mission continued its growth. The soup kitchen and poor man's dining hall in Whitechapel offered cheap and nutritious meals to over two thousand men and women. People flocked to the reading rooms and other warm and comfortable places the mission provided as an alternative to the pubs.

Throughout this time Catherine kept on preaching in churches around England, and William wrote a short book entitled *How to Reach the Masses With the Gospel: A Sketch of the Origin, History and Present Position of the Christian Mission.* In this book he set out his ideas on preaching the gospel and the opposition those who tried to reach the poor would face. He warned:

> This kind of work ensures opposition and persecution, it raises the hatred of men and devils.... If you will stop quietly in your church or chapel or meeting place, you may talk of religion forever and, beyond a little passing ridicule, the ungodly will let you alone.... Only proclaim the truth at the gates of the city or in the crowded market place and they will gnash upon you with their teeth and

> hate you as they hated Him [Jesus] who went about all the cities and villages in Palestine.

As if to prove William's point, the East London Christian Mission continued to be embroiled in very public persecution. Catholics in Croydon threw pots at mission workers, while in the East End the workers were pelted with flour, mud, stones, and cabbage stalks. In Shoreditch, drunk men threatened to punch any man or woman who spoke the name of Jesus.

One confrontation, which made newspaper headlines, became know as the Battle of Sanger's Circus. The circus set itself up near one of the mission's preaching stations. This was a double insult to William, since he objected to circuses because he believed that they were cruel to animals and that the circus had more "star power" than a preacher did. At the Battle of Sanger's Circus, the preacher announced a hymn, which he and his helpers started singing loudly. Soon circus employees started pelting the singers with clods of dirt and stones. The group sang on. Next the circus brought out several brass instruments, and the clowns and acrobats made an awful din with them. The group started on a new song, "I Am a Pilgrim, Bound for Glory." Since the tuba and trumpet were having little effect, more instruments appeared. A huge drum was beat, and a pretty girl bashed cymbals behind the preacher. All of this drew an immense crowd of onlookers. It was much more entertaining than either the preaching or the circus. Not to be defeated, the circus brought out its star attractions—a large elephant and two dromedaries! The animals' handlers led the animals into the crowd. Men shouted and women screamed and grabbed their children as the animals swayed by. But the preacher continued on.

An hour and a half later the group sang their final hymn and invited people in the crowd to come forward and become Christians. The mission had triumphed in the true style of William Booth.

Confrontations like these made both the workers and the converts bolder than ever. Many poor people embroidered Bible verses they could not even read onto their clothing, and a chair mender changed his chant from "Bring out your broken chairs to mend" to "Bring out your broken hearts to mend."

A new headquarters at 272 Whitechapel Road meant that some of the East London Christian Mission papers were moved out of the Booths' house and the children were able to spread out a little more. However, it was a constant strain finding people who could read and write well enough to help staff the new headquarters. At one point William had only a young boy and an ex-cook to handle all the paperwork. Debts were often left unpaid, and urgent letters slipped behind the mail desk. Whenever possible, William's oldest children were pressed into service, but even they could not keep up with the growing work. What William needed was a private secretary, though he had no idea where to find one.

Chapter 9

Introducing the Salvation Army

It was a cool autumn day in 1872 when William Booth eased his tired body into a warm mineral bath at Matlock. When he felt ill, William often came to the baths to relax his aching joints and enjoy the quiet atmosphere. He had just settled onto a wooden seat at the edge of the bath when the proprietor, Mr. Smedley, walked in, escorting a stranger to the pool that William was in. As soon as he saw William, he stopped and smiled. "Ha, the Reverend William Booth," he said. "May I introduce you to the Reverend Launcelot Railton. You should have a lot in common to talk about. The Reverend Railton is a Methodist minister."

William nodded as Mr. Railton climbed down the stone steps and into the bath.

"Are you *the* Reverend William Booth of the East London Christian Mission?" Launcelot Railton asked nervously in his Scottish brogue.

"That is I," William replied. "How have you come to hear of me?"

The Reverend Railton swirled the water with his hand, waiting a long time to reply. "My younger brother George speaks of you," he said disapprovingly. "He has read some of your pamphlets and finds himself in agreement with your methods."

"He does?" William said. "Do I take it from your tone of voice that you do not?"

Launcelot Railton took a deep breath. "If you had been subjected to the antics of my younger brother, you would be less than willing to give him any encouragement. Really, it's hard to imagine he will ever grow into a responsible adult. He's twenty-three, but he has the harebrained notions of a thirteen-year-old!"

"How so?" William asked, his curiosity piqued.

"Well, there is his infamous trip to Morocco. I am not against missions, sir. Let me tell you that our parents were missionaries to Antigua before George was born. But George does everything to extreme. He took all the money he had to his name—a grand sum of twenty pounds—and bought a steamship ticket to Morocco. When he got there, he made a banner that read, 'Repentance, Faith, Holiness,' and walked the marketplaces holding it high above his head." The Reverend Railton paused for a moment before he went on. "Of course he ran out of money in the end, but he kept parading that foolish banner, with nowhere to stay and no food to eat. Thank goodness the British consul got wind of his predicament and insisted he stop making such an exhibition of himself and shipped him back to England on the first available steamer."

"He sounds like a dedicated young man!" William said. "What is he doing now?"

Launcelot Railton snickered. "He's living in Middlesbrough, preaching every Sunday in, of all things, a butcher's shop! He goes in after the shop is closed on Saturday afternoon and scrubs down the chopping block so that he can use it as a pulpit. Can you imagine that?" He looked at William and continued dryly. "Well, I imagine you can! He talks of becoming a Methodist minister, but I doubt we would take him on. Far too radical…unbalanced, really."

The two men then sat in silence, steam from the bath wafting up between them.

In the weeks that followed, William often thought back to the conversation and wondered about George Railton and his efforts at evangelism. Just after New Year's, he found out firsthand. It was late at night, and William had just finished preaching when a young man waving a copy of *How to Reach the Masses* emerged from the crowd.

"I have to talk to you, Reverend Booth!" the young man called to William. "I have read this book many times, and I am convinced you and your East London Christian Missionaries are the people for me."

William studied the young man as he pushed through the crowd to the front. The young man, who was tall and stocky with piercing blue eyes and an auburn beard, took off his hat when he reached William. "Allow me to introduce myself," he said. "I am George Railton."

"Would you be the brother of the Reverend Launcelot Railton?" William asked.

The young man stepped back. "Yes," he said, and then added hastily, "but we have very differing views on missionary work."

"I am sure you do," William said. "Tell me, George, where are you staying tonight?"

"I don't have anywhere particular in mind," George replied.

"Then you must come and meet my wife and spend the night with us," William said.

William and George walked back to the Booth home on Gore Road together. George talked enthusiastically most of the way, explaining that William's pamphlet had convinced him he belonged among the East London Christian Mission workers.

William had meant for George to stay at his house for only a few days, but much to his surprise he discovered that the young man had an amazing knack for office work. Within a week George had rearranged the filing system for the mission's office and put the regular bills in order. As William watched

George work, he knew one thing—he had found the private secretary he so desperately needed.

The two youngest Booth children were moved into the attic. George was then given their bedroom as his own and a hearty welcome into the noisy Booth household, which by now included not only a dog but also white mice, guinea pigs, birds, and even a pet monkey named Little Jeannie.

Within a short time George understood William's ideas on evangelism, especially the notion that it was not money that would reach the poor masses in England. Only the poor themselves, motivated by the love and power of God, could do that. The East London Christian Mission's job was to mobilize the poor to reach out to each other. Understanding this, George was able to help write the hundreds of letters that took up much of William's time. He also threw his enthusiasm behind the mission's small newsletter, now called the *Christian Mission Magazine.* Within a year the publication had doubled in size and subscriptions.

William tried not to dictate the tone of the magazine, and soon George was sprinkling it with military terms. The Civil War in America had ended eight years before, but it was still fresh enough in the public's mind to give military words and phrases an air of excitement. So instead of writing about opening a new preaching station at Southsea Common, George wrote about "the opening of a new battery of artillery on Southsea Common" that would no doubt "develop into a regiment." William approved of these phrases when he read them and even more so of a new song George published, entitled "Our War Song."

George also reported on the many new developments in the mission. Some of them happened so quickly that it was difficult for William to keep up with them all. There was a new Whitechapel People's Hall, seating two thousand people, while a beerhouse and brewery in Stoke Newington were purchased and turned into a preaching center. And on Bethnal Green permission was granted for a huge railway arch to be bricked in and the space used for evangelism. Other branches of the mission were opened in Hastings, Tunbridge Wells, and Northumberland. It was obvious that the East London Christian Mission was reaching out and "occupying much enemy territory." The mission also expanded into the poorest cities of Wales.

During this time of exhilarating expansion, one sad event occurred. In January 1875 William's mother, Mary, died after being bedridden for several years following a fall. Even though she was eighty-four years old, William felt sure she could have lived much longer had it not been for the accident. His sister Emma had died four years earlier, leaving only his sister Mary alive.

By 1876 William and the mission were recruiting an ever-growing number of converts, and because of this, William was always on the lookout for potential evangelists. On a warm night in August he had just finished preaching at the Whitechapel

People's Hall when he came face-to-face with one of the most dynamic men he had ever met. The man introduced himself as "Fiery Elijah" Cadman, and he immediately reminded William of a coiled watch spring—ready to burst forth at any moment. He was wearing a well-cut suit and a tall silk hat, but those symbols of middle-class respectability did not hide his cockney accent.

"You might have heard about me," Elijah told William. "Around Warwickshire I'm known as 'The Saved Sweep from Rugby.'"

"Is that so?" William replied. "Tell me more."

Soon the two men were sitting on a bench, where Elijah poured out his story. His father had hired him at age six to a chimney sweep, and at 4 A.M. each day, Elijah donned a calico mask and was hoisted up some well-to-do person's fireplace to scrape the soot off the insides of the chimney. It was frightening work for a young child, and Elijah often lost his footing and crashed down into the fire grate below. From the very beginning, his employer paid him with beer, and Elijah seldom went home sober.

At eighteen years of age, Elijah was far too large to climb around inside chimneys, and he had turned to a life of prize boxing to feed himself. During that time he went to see a public hanging at the Warwick jail. As he saw the criminal swaying from the hangman's noose, he was struck by the thought that if he did not change his ways, he could well face the same fate. Without any further prompting, Elijah surrendered his life to God and set about preaching to his friends. Over time he had married and built up a small business. His brother-in-law told him about William Booth, and Elijah declared that he was anxious to join the mission.

William listened carefully to all the young man had to say and then invited him to preach at a meeting in Wellingborough. The event was a wonderful success. William was astonished at how well this short, stocky man could hold an audience spellbound—especially after he "read" from an upside-down Bible. It turned out that Elijah could not read a word but had memorized large portions of Scripture to preach from and would hold an open Bible up to give the illusion that he was reading from it. He did not always hold it up the right way, however. As he preached, he was in constant motion, even straddling the penitent rail as he made the point that it is difficult to sit on the fence, being a Christian but not one who truly puts God first in his or her life. Just as he had with George Railton, William soon became convinced that Elijah Cadman would prove to be a special asset to the mission.

Just over a year later, in October 1877, Elijah was preaching in the small Yorkshire town of Whitby. William took the train north to visit him there. When he arrived, he found that "Captain Cadman," as he now called himself, was "waging war with the Hallelujah Army" and that he had over three thousand followers. William was most impressed with this, and he soon noticed how much the poorest fishermen and factory workers rallied to the same sort of military language George Railton had introduced in the mission's magazine. Posters around town announced, "WAR! WAR! 200 MEN AND WOMEN WANTED AT ONCE TO JOIN THE HALLELUJAH ARMY." Another read, "THE MIDDLESBRO' ARTILLERY IS TO ARRIVE AT 9:30 A.M. WITH THEIR BIG GUNS...AND HOSPITAL FOR THE WOUNDED AND ALL WHO WANT TO BE HEALED FROM SIN."

William found one more poster stuffed behind a radiator in Elijah's parlor. It was the most startling of all. In large red letters it declared, "COME AND HEAR THE GENERAL OF THE HALLELUJAH ARMY!" As soon as Elijah returned, William asked him about the hidden poster. "What does it mean?"

Elijah looked nervous, an expression William had never seen on his face before. "I...I...didn't put it up, Reverend Booth. Really, I didn't. It was just that I got carried away with calling myself a captain and all, and I decided you should be called the general." He gave William a sheepish glance. "But then I thought better of it."

"Why?" William asked, warming to the idea. "A Hallelujah Army should have a general, and after all, my title is already General Superintendent of the East London Christian Mission. Go right ahead and put the poster up if you think it will draw a crowd. I would be honored to lead the troops right into the devil's encampment! And while you are at it, send a copy of the poster to George Railton. I think he would enjoy the idea of me being a general. Let me see; that would make him my lieutenant."

"Are you sure?" Elijah asked.

"Positive!" William replied. "Drawing a crowd, that's the first thing. If calling me General Booth helps you do that, then as far as I'm concerned, that's my name."

And so it was. Word quickly spread that William Booth had taken on the mantle of general, and many other mission workers followed Elijah Cadman in billing themselves as captains in the fight for God. This change in title was just the first of many important changes that were to take place over the next eighteen months.

Around 7 A.M. one morning in May 1878, William was holding a meeting in his bedroom. He had the flu, and he did not feel well enough to go downstairs. However, he needed to go over the proofs of the mission's annual report and had invited George Railton and Bramwell to his bedroom to do so.

From his bed William read the front page of the document aloud over George's shoulder. "The Christian mission, under the superintendence of the Rev. William Booth, is a volunteer army."

"Volunteer!" Bramwell exclaimed. "I am not a volunteer. I am a regular or nothing!"

William lay silently in his bed. If *volunteer* was not the right word, what was? A thought flashed through his mind, and he plucked the pen from George's hand and crossed out the word *volunteer*. Then he wrote in big, bold letters: "SALVATION."

"We shall be known as the Salvation Army," he said.

At his word Bramwell and George leaped from their chairs and yelled in unison, "Thank God for that."

Chapter 10

"Unbecoming and Extreme"

The Salvation Army was born in May 1878. News of its founding fired the imagination of many of the old East London Christian Mission workers, and soon military words and phrases were popping up everywhere. Captain Cadman had often called his Bible a "sword," and now many others followed his example. Large mission houses were referred to as "citadels" and smaller ones as "forts." Groups of workers called themselves "troops," who together made up a "corps." Everyone wanted a rank: Part-time workers over fifteen years of age became soldiers, and full-time workers became officers. When they preached, the captains opened with shouts of "Fire a volley," which meant for the audience to shout out a stirring hallelujah, and when it was time to pray, everyone was to do "knee-drill." Bible reading became "taking rations." The *Christian Mission Magazine* was renamed *The War Cry,* and a second magazine was published for children and called *Little Soldiers*.

Any army had to have uniforms, and soon the men were wearing plain blue serge suits with a brass letter 'S' on the collar and a bold red shirt underneath. The women wore a discreet navy skirt and jacket with a black straw bonnet. Catherine Booth designed the bonnet with a tilted brim to deflect flying missiles. This quickly became known as the Hallelujah Bonnet. William Booth took to carrying an umbrella and wearing a black top hat and a long frock coat that made him look like a veteran of the American Civil War.

William came up with the pattern for the Salvation Army flag. It had a red background, representing the blood of Jesus, a blue border, representing the holiness of God, and a yellow sun that represented the fire of the Holy Spirit. The new motto, "Blood and Fire," was emblazoned across it. The flag was often carried into "battle" while the troops sang, "Onward, Christian soldiers, / Marching as to war, / With the cross of Jesus / Going on before: / Christ the royal Master / Leads against the foe; / Forward into battle, / See, His banners go!"

All of these changes captured the imagination of the poor, who flocked as never before to hear the gospel preached. One year after the Salvation Army was born, the number of army units had risen from twenty-nine to eighty-one. There were now 127 officers, where there had been only thirty-one full-time workers in the old East London Christian Mission. Best of all, as far as William was concerned, these new officers were "homegrown." Over one hundred of them had been converted through the work of the mission and were now eager to serve others. And there was plenty of work for them all to do, as an estimated twenty-seven thousand soldiers and seekers came to Sunday night meetings in citadels and forts around the United Kingdom.

William's children were a part of the Salvation Army from the very first day. Thirteen-year-old Eva even recruited Little Jeannie, their pet monkey. She made her a tiny army uniform, complete with insignia. When Catherine saw it, she quietly took the uniform off Little Jeannie and looked sternly at her daughter.

"Why can't she wear it?" Eva asked sullenly.

"Because she doesn't live the life!" Catherine replied. "A man may be changed, but once a monkey, always a monkey."

William laughed heartily when he heard of this escapade. There was no doubt his family revolved around this new army. In fact, his children sold more copies of *The War Cry* than anyone else. They developed a system that always "pressed the advantage," as William's father used to say. Before they took to the streets, the children would read the current issue through carefully. They then made a list of all the counties and towns mentioned in its articles and committed the list to memory before heading to Liverpool Street Station. When a train came in, they took note of where it was from and yelled out some piece of news reported in *The War Cry* that had occurred there. Inevitably a traveler's interest would be piqued by news of the place the traveler had just come from, and wanting to know more, the traveler bought the paper.

As the converts poured into the Salvation Army, many of them expressed their new faith in strange and wonderful ways. A converted drunk who did a show that involved Houdini-like escapes now donned the army uniform and drew a crowd by combining his contortionist talents with a sermon entitled "Trap Doors to Hell." Captain Lawley got so worked up during one of his sermons that he dived off the platform and landed belly-first on the floor, where he did the breaststroke and continued preaching on the boundless sea of God's love. Another soldier, who had been in the Royal Navy, wore an outfit that reflected both his past and his present life. The outfit was sewed down the middle, with the left side of his body dressed as a sailor and the right side in the Salvation Army uniform. Anyone who asked about his peculiar attire got a minisermon on the spot.

Soldiers and captains competed for the best way to draw a crowd. Bramwell Booth sometimes climbed into a coffin and was carried along the streets to St. Paul's by six men. Once they reached the steps of the great cathedral, he popped out of the coffin and preached on the text "O death, where is thy sting?" Another man, who lacked any kind of acting talent, decided to lie silently in the snow near a local marketplace. After doing this for five evenings, many people came to look at him. This provided him with the crowd he needed to preach to about how God could thaw the coldest heart.

William did not worry about what the "respectable" newspapers were calling "unbecoming and extreme" behavior. He was happy to see almost any method used to attract the attention of potential converts. Surprisingly, about the only attention-getting device he did not consider proper was music. William believed that using loud instruments, particularly when the gospel was about to be preached, undermined the sacred atmosphere. Somehow he failed to see that music was not nearly as distracting as many of the other antics that went on!

However, in July 1879 William traveled to Salisbury to speak in a series of open-air rallies. There he was introduced to a local builder named Will Fry. Will had three sons, Fred, Ernest, and Bert, who along with their father had volunteered to act as bodyguards for Salvation Army officers during the meetings, since hooligans had threatened to disrupt them. The Frys were all talented musicians, and since they did not know that William objected to musical accompaniment, they brought their brass instruments along to the rallies to help boost the singing.

William was astonished at how many people the brass quartet attracted, and he knew it was time to rethink his ideas on music. He hired the Frys to play each night, and William had some of the best ever results from his preaching during this time. That settled it in his mind. He gave the brass band concept official approval, and soon corps all over England were tuning up their instruments.

To the musically trained ear much of what the early Salvation Army produced sounded awful. Old beat-up instruments were dragged out of attics or bought from pawnshops. Many of these instruments were held together with wire or had leaks plugged with soap. However, they all had one thing in common—they all made noise. Many soldiers who could not read words learned to read musical notes. To give them clues as to the name of the tune, the sheets of music had pictures instead of titles at the top of them. A person wanting to play "Out on the Ocean Sailing" merely had to look for the sheet with the boat on it.

It seemed that everyone wanted to play something—even those with no obvious talent. Tambourines with ribbons flailing became an early favorite, as did bells borrowed from dustmen. Within a year there were four hundred Salvation Army bands crashing and blowing their way along the streets of England's industrial cities.

Along with the band music came a flurry of new songs. Most of them were adaptations of popular pub songs, and William once again was not sure of this trend. But when he heard George "Sailor" Fielder sing "Bless His Name, He Sets Me Free" at a theatre in Worchester, William found himself humming along to the catchy tune. When the song was finished, he turned to the officer beside him and said, "What a rousing song that is. What is the tune?"

"Oh," the officer replied, "that's 'Champagne Charlie Is My Name.'"

William thought for a minute or two and then turned to Bramwell. "That settles it. Why should the devil have all the best tunes?"

An army needed training barracks, and these came in the form of the Booths' home in Hackney. The family moved into a sixteen-room house on the edge of Clapton Common in East London, and their Gore Street home became a place to train "cadets." Thirty young women were taken in to be trained under Emma Booth, who was herself only twenty years old. Soon another house was rented in Hackney, and a men's training barracks was set up under the command of Captain Ballington Booth.

Both the men's and the women's courses lasted for seven weeks, and the training was one hundred percent practical. Cadets rose at dawn to a meager breakfast of bread and weak tea, and then they scrubbed the barracks and polished their boots. By eight o'clock they were visiting the slums, where they picked lice out of children's hair, scrubbed filthy rooms clean, and hand-fed senile men. As they worked, they sang or shared the gospel message.

One by one, each of the younger Booth children went through the cadet training course, and the creativity with which they shared the gospel inspired many others. Of course, they had lived with the general all their lives and watched his many innovations. But one day Eva managed to confound even her father.

William was sitting in his office when his secretary announced there was a very distraught young flower seller who wanted to see him. "Show her in," he replied, putting the lid on his fountain pen.

In walked a tall, bony girl wearing a tattered dress, worn boots, and darned stockings. Her hair hung over her face. She looked just like the other flower sellers who hawked their wares around the fountain at Piccadilly Circus. Tears were streaming down her face.

"Come, come, young lady, don't cry," William said. "Tell me what is troubling you, and I'll do what I can to help."

This led to more sobbing. Then after a moment or two the girl recovered enough to speak. "I…I was walking down a side street when I was robbed of my flower basket. It was full, I was just going off to work, and now I don't know what to do." She sobbed some more. "If I go home without any money, my stepfather will beat me."

William felt sorry for the girl standing in front of him. He knew how difficult life was for girls like her. He reached into his pocket and pulled out some coins. Just then he heard laughter. "Oh, Father, don't you know me!" exclaimed the girl.

"Eva?" William said incredulously. Eva's costume and makeup were so expertly done that he didn't even recognize his own daughter! He laughed heartily. "You fooled me that time," he said. "What are you doing dressed as a flower seller?"

"I am having the most wonderful time," Eva told him. "I've been selling flowers and working among the girls who work near me. They accept me as one of their own, and they let me help them and give them advice, though sometimes I get advice too."

"What sort of advice?" William asked.

"The other day I was walking down a back alley. I was limping, and an old man approached me. 'You don't look well,' he said. 'I think you should go and get help at the Salvation Army.' So I replied, 'Do you think they'd be able to do anything for the likes of me?' And do you know what he said, Father? You would have loved to hear this. He said, 'I was worse than you. I was a real bad egg. They took me by the hand and pulled me up. You go to them straightaway, lass. They'll help you. Don't be afraid.'"

William grinned from ear to ear. No wonder the Salvation Army was growing so fast; the poor were recommending it to one another.

Of course, Eva was not the only one doing such things. Many of the other cadets were employing similar antics as they sought to proclaim the gospel.

A good many pastors, though, thought the cadet training program could not be considered a proper Bible training school without an emphasis on subjects like Greek and Latin. When they were brave enough to say this to his face, William always replied,

"We say, teach the builder how to build houses, the shoemaker how to make shoes, and the soul winner *how to win souls.* We try to train the mind so that it is a little ahead in intelligence and information of the people to whom they minister. This means we teach cadets who need it reading, writing, and arithmetic and the basics of history and geography."

William was happy to see the work in the United Kingdom growing so rapidly, but he was reluctant to be involved in anything beyond her shores. During Christmastime 1879 he found an envelope from America in his daily mail dispatch from George Railton. As William opened the letter, a newspaper clipping from the *Philadelphia News Report* fluttered to the floor. He picked it up and read it.

The clipping told how an Amos Shirley, along with his wife, Anne, and their daughter Eliza, had set up two Salvation Army corps in Philadelphia. William was stunned as he read. The article said the Shirleys had emigrated from Coventry, England, where they had been members of the local Salvation Army corps, to work in Philadelphia. On arriving in their adopted land, Anne and Eliza soon became known in local newspapers as the "Two Hallelujah Females." But their efforts attracted a large enough crowd to justify renting an old chair factory in which to preach and then a second preaching hall off Market Street.

Once he had read the article, William unfolded the accompanying letter from Amos Shirley. In the letter Amos begged the general to visit Philadelphia and give the work in America his official Salvation Army blessing. At the bottom of the letter George had scribbled the comment, "We must go. This news has come upon us like a voice from Heaven and leaves us no choice."

William was not so convinced. America was a long way away, and he had tried not to open any station he could not personally oversee. However, George was sure that this was the right move, and he first convinced Catherine, and then William, of it. Once William decided to act, he was not one to waste time. He rejected the idea of going to America himself, though, as there was simply too much going on in England. When George asked to be sent in his place, William agreed.

On January 12, 1880, eight officers ready to "open fire" in America paraded outside the Whitechapel headquarters. They consisted of George Railton, six Hallelujah Lassies, and Emma Westbrook, the Booths' red-haired cook, who had become soundly converted and joined the army. Emma went along to act as a chaperone for the young women. Catherine Booth presented the group with two flags, one for the Philadelphia battalion and the other for a New York battalion that George intended to set up after he had visited the Shirleys.

As William said good-bye to the man who had become like a son to him, he advised George, "Never forget that it is not what you do yourself as much as what you get others to do that will be the making of the army."

Soon afterward the determined group marched aboard the SS *Australia,* bound for New York City.

In many ways George Railton could not have left William at a worse time. The Salvation Army was growing exponentially and attracting a lot of attention both from people who admired their work and from those who hated it. William had even been told that Queen Victoria objected to the Salvation Army on the grounds that she should have the only army in England and that all generals should belong to the British Empire. And Lord Shaftsbury—along with many members of England's upper class—was terrified of what the Salvation Army might do. He saw it as a militant force, dressed in uniform, using fighting language, and determined to tear apart the established order of English society. On Sundays these rich and powerful people went to church and sang hymns like the very popular "All Things Bright and Beautiful." The first verse was very cheery:

> Each little flower that opens,
> Each little bird that sings,
> He made their glowing colors,
> He made their tiny wings.

The second verse to the hymn went like this:

> The rich man in his castle,
> The poor man at his gate,
> He made them, high or lowly,
> And ordered their estate.

No one questioned the implications of the verse because it was the common belief that God put everyone in his or her social class, and as long as poor people—even starving people—accepted that, all would be right in God's England. Many people in the upper classes of English society feared that the Salvation Army was about to wage a class war in much the same way that communists were inciting peasants to rise up in other parts of Europe. This led to a strange alliance among many influential church leaders, politicians, local hoodlums, and brewery owners, all of whom wanted the Salvation Army to march right out of sight.

From the time William had first started preaching among the poor, he had been pelted with rotten vegetables and clods of dirt. But now things had become much uglier. Bands and preachers were pelted with bricks, sticks, stones, and even dead cats.

Things came to a head one Monday in January 1882. The Salvation Army was holding its annual Council of War in Sheffield, and Elijah Cadman had organized a march through town to Albert Hall, where a holiness meeting was to be held. Leading the parade was a brass band mounted on a wagon pulled by four white horses. Behind the band, mounted on a white horse, was Lieutenant Emmerson Davidson, a champion Northumberland wrestler. Behind him came William and Catherine riding in an open carriage. And behind them were scores of Salvation Army members clad in neat uniforms and arranged by rank. They carried flags and banners proclaiming who they were and what their mission was.

As the procession made its way through the streets, a large crowd gathered to watch. Among the crowd were about a thousand local hoodlums who called themselves the Sheffield Blades. Suddenly one of the hoodlums hurled a short, thick stick. The stick hit Lieutenant Davidson low on the back of his head. The lieutenant slumped forward, fighting to stay conscious and keep from tumbling to the cobbled street. Two young men from the crowd rushed forward and tried to pull him down. One pulled from the left side and the other from the right. Their efforts seemed to counteract each other, and Emmerson Davidson stayed on his horse. Finally several Salvation Army officers rushed forward and chased the two hoodlums off. They then marched alongside Lieutenant Davidson, steadying him on his horse.

At the same time, clods of mud began to hail down on the band at the front of the procession. The band tried to keep playing, but as more and more mud descended on them from the crowd, followed by rotten vegetables, eggs, and finally dead cats, they faltered.

Seeing what was happening ahead of him, William stood up in his carriage to encourage his soldiers. The same missiles were aimed at him, but William stood his ground.

By now the local hoodlums had rushed forward and were attacking those behind William's carriage, trying to pull down their flags and banners. Scuffles broke out as Salvation Army soldiers struggled to keep hold of their banners.

"Stay near the carriage! Stay near the carriage!" William exhorted.

As Salvation Army soldiers moved in tight around his carriage, the city police joined their ranks. Members of the band, their uniforms muddied, began to pass their now battered instruments back to William's carriage for safekeeping as abusive men hurled themselves at the marchers.

Finally, as Albert Hall came into view, Elijah Cadman made his way from the rear of the procession to William's carriage. His nose was broken and his face was bloodied, but his spirit remained unbowed by the riot going on around him. William asked Elijah if the officers were all right. In true Salvation Army style, Elijah replied, "The officers will be all right, dead or alive!"

Eventually all those in the procession made it to relative safety inside Albert Hall as the police barred the way of the hoodlums who were intent on pursuing members of the Salvation Army inside and causing more trouble. (Now unconscious, Lieutenant Davidson was slid off his horse and taken to a nearby hospital, where he stayed for several weeks, recovering from a severe concussion.)

Inside Albert Hall, William rose to address the gathered crowd. Instead of the sermon he had planned to preach, he spoke about the riot that had just taken place. "Here, publicly, I want to forgive those who so rudely attacked me outside. They are men in desperate need of the Savior's love, and that is what I want to extend to them."

William also exhorted his soldiers not to lose heart and instead to wear every wound as a badge of honor and courage. They would need his exhortation and encouragement in the months ahead because the riot in Sheffield would not be the last one in England to erupt around Salvation Army rallies.

Chapter 11

The Skeleton Army

Although the police in Sheffield had attempted to protect William during the riot there, no one was ever charged in the disturbance. As the months went on, it became obvious to William that the police department's will to protect the Salvation Army was weakening. In fact, the British Home Secretary pushed for a peace-at-any-price policy. This meant that the results of any legal Salvation Army activity that hooligans turned into a riot were blamed on the Salvation Army. The Home Secretary's logic went thus: If the Salvation Army had not been there in the first place, the peace would not have been disturbed.

Because they knew they could get away with it, many angry and restless young men began organizing themselves into groups whose stated aim was to destroy the Salvation Army. They called themselves a Skeleton Army, after the skull-and-crossbones flag they adopted as their banner. Some branches of the Skeleton Army even held special sessions to teach their members how to more accurately hurl projectiles at Salvation Army soldiers as they gathered in the street. And they didn't confine their harassment to Salvation Army groups they encountered in the streets. They attacked buildings the Salvation Army owned or used or the homes of anyone who sympathized with the organization, smashing windows and hurling dead cats and rats, bricks, stones, vegetables, and sticks inside. On one occasion at Weston-super-Mare, a group of Skeleton Army men smashed the windows of the Salvation Army citadel during a service and let a flock of pigeons inside. The Skeleton Army had placed red pepper under the pigeons' wings so that, as the frightened birds fluttered around, the pepper rained down on those inside the hall. Gasping for air, their noses and eyes running, those inside ran out, right into the arms of the waiting Skeleton Army, who savagely beat them.

To make matters worse, the Skeleton Army was often financially supported in its efforts by breweries and pub owners, and magistrates outraged by the Salvation Army's unorthodox approach to proclaiming the gospel were also sympathetic to its cause.

When scuffles broke out, it was always the Salvation Army officers who were arrested for disorderly conduct. Things continued to deteriorate until, in 1882, six hundred sixty-nine Salvation Army soldiers were badly hurt in assaults, many of them while they were preaching in their own halls and citadels, and sixty buildings were torn apart. All of this happened under the disinterested gaze of the British police, who in some instances joined in to help the Skeleton Army.

In the midst of this, William received terrible news. One of his first converts from the East End of London, Susannah Beaty, had been killed. She was a captain in the city of Hastings, and during a procession she had been pelted with rotten fish and rocks. One of the rocks knocked her off her feet, and as she lay in the street, a thug kicked her hard in the stomach. She died from internal injuries.

William needed all the help he could get in fighting this threat to the existence of the Salvation Army. He wrote to George Railton to ask him to return from the United States and help at headquarters in London. He also wrote many letters to members of Parliament and other government leaders, urging them to set aside the peace-at-any-price policy. Next he called for the police to protect all citizens who were acting in a legal manner, especially since the death of Susannah Beaty only seemed to embolden the Skeleton Army in their attacks.

Finally the tide of apathy about protecting members of the Salvation Army turned in Worthing, Sussex, where Ada Smith, a petite Salvation Army captain, faced vicious opposition. Undeterred, Ada encouraged her corps of twenty men and women to stand firm in the face of the onslaught of a Skeleton Army of over four thousand thugs. To make matters worse, the local newspaper had inflamed public opinion by calling Ada Smith and her soldiers "excitable young men and hysterical young women who mistake a quasi-religious revelry for godliness." As well, Worthing's police surgeon had offered a twenty-pound reward to the first person to throw one of the Hallelujah Lassies into the sea. When William heard of the persecution the Worthing corps was enduring, he wrote to the British Home Office asking that the Home Secretary insist the police protect them from the hooligans. The Home Secretary replied that he did not have the necessary power over local governments to order the police to do so.

Eventually four thousand angry men descended on the small band of Salvation Army soldiers, pelting them with rocks and tar. When a few police officers arrived at the scene, the leader of the Skeleton Army assaulted one of the officers. The man was immediately arrested. It was one thing to attack a nineteen-year-old Salvation Army girl, but quite another to assault a policeman. As the leader was dragged away, the Skeleton Army turned its fury on the police force, throwing rocks into the police station and taunting the officers to come out. Finally the Worthing police saw the truth of the matter. It was impossible to ignore the rights of one group of people and allow thugs to roam the streets without putting everyone's liberty at risk. They began a crackdown on the Skeleton Army, and soon other police forces followed their example, not wanting four thousand rioting thugs in their districts.

In the midst of these trials, the Salvation Army kept growing, until it needed a larger home. In 1882 it entered negotiations to buy the old London Orphan Asylum. The original cost of the building had been sixty thousand pounds, but William was delighted when the price was reduced to fifteen thousand pounds so that the Army could purchase it. He renamed the building Clapton Congress Hall, and it became the National Barracks or Training Garrison.

During this time the Booth children grew more useful in their service to the Salvation Army and its general. Twenty-three-year-old Kate was sent to Paris to "open fire" there. This was a difficult task, especially since Paris was a hotbed of communism and the main religion was not Protestantism but Catholicism. But William was convinced that his fiery, auburn-haired daughter was the right person to send to establish the Salvation Army's beachhead in Europe. When people came to him asking if he thought it was wise to send a single woman into such a rough situation, he always offered the same reply, "Kate knows the Lord." He knew that out of all his children, Kate was the one most like him in determination and courage.

On October 12, 1882, Bramwell Booth married Captain Florence Soper before a crowd of six thousand members of the Salvation Army. William led the marriage service and listened to the couple's promise, which was made to the Salvation Army. It came straight from the "Articles of Marriage," which he had recently drawn up for his troops. The promise stated, "We promise never to allow our marriage to lessen in any way our devotion to God and the Army and to regard and arrange our home as a Salvation Army officer's home."

Thinking of the Salvation Army first, William had insisted that the wedding guests pay a one-shilling admission fee, the money going toward the purchase of a pub called the Eagle Tavern. This pub was so notorious that a children's rhyme had been made up about it:

> Up and down the city road,
> In and out the Eagle,
> That's the way the money goes,
> Pop goes the weasel.

The word *pop* was slang for pawning something, and *weasel* was slang for a watch. So the rhyme was really a reminder of how many times men and women pawned their earthly goods to drink at the Eagle Tavern.

At the end of 1882, William surveyed the Salvation Army reports. There were now 440 Salvation Army corps worldwide, with 1,019 officers. Also, ten thousand copies of *The War Cry* were printed and distributed each month. More astonishing was the fact that the Salvation Army now "occupied" five continents. An Australian corps was established in much the same way the United States corps had been established. Harry Saunders, a butcher from Bradford, had immigrated to Adelaide and joined with a few others, including John Gore, "the happy milkman," to set up a corps. The work grew rapidly, and soon they were writing to William to introduce themselves and ask for reinforcements.

A colonial judge named Fredrick Tucker had begun the work of the Salvation Army in India. He was an Indian language scholar, and while serving in Amritsar, India, he had read a copy of *The War Cry* and decided to join the organization. He and his wife traveled to London to meet William, and then in 1882 they, along with several other Army officers, "opened fire" in India.

With so much growth, the money to pay officers their meager salaries and fund the work always seemed to be lagging. One day, in a conversation with Major John Carlton, a chance remark gave William an idea about raising more money for the work of the Salvation Army.

"If I go without my pudding every day for a year," John said, "I calculate I will save fifty shillings. And I will remit that money to the army."

William's face lit up. "Now there's an idea," he said. "It might be a bit much to ask our soldiers to go without pudding for a whole year, but I can see no reason why we shouldn't ask them to unite in going without something every day for a week and give the money they save to the work of the Salvation Army."

And so Self-Denial Week was born. Members of the Salvation Army in Great Britain were asked to forego something for a week and give the money they saved to the army. Even William, who by now existed on a diet of soup, cheese, baked apples, and rice pudding, made his own diet still more scant. Penny by penny money rolled in, until at the end of the week, 4,820 pounds had been raised.

Many opponents of the Salvation Army criticized William for asking his workers to deny themselves to save some portion of their meager income to give back to the army. They predicted it was an act of desperation and that the Salvation Army would soon be out of business. These critics were soon proved wrong as the Salvation Army continued to grow and Self-Denial Week went on to become the army's major fundraising drive each year.

On a crisp spring morning in May 1885, William walked into the Salvation Army headquarters on Queen Victoria Street. He was drinking his first cup of tea for the day when Bramwell burst into his office. "General, we have to do something. The most extraordinary thing happened this morning, and I don't think we should let it rest. It's time for war!"

"Wait a minute!" William replied. "Slow down and start at the beginning."

Bramwell paced as he spoke. "A seventeen-year-old girl was waiting on the doorstep this morning. She said her name was Annie Swan, and she came from Shoreham, Sussex." He sat down, then promptly stood up again and kept pacing. "She told Major Fenny and then me that her parents had arranged for her to come to London to work as a parlor maid for a family. But when she went to the address, she was taken inside, given a red blouse and skirt to put on, and locked up. Can you believe that? What a dreadful trick! Thankfully she'd been to a Salvation Army meeting back in Sussex and still carried with her the songbook she had been given there. At two o'clock this morning she took the songbook and managed to escape. Using the address on the back, she found her way here and waited for the door to be opened."

"What do you think, Bramwell? What should we do?" William asked.

Bramwell's eyes were burning like firebrands. "General," he said, "we have read the debates that have been going on in Parliament about situations like this, but nothing has happened. Someone was on our doorstep asking for help. Now it's time to act! Besides, it's outrageous that girls as young as thirteen can enter this horrible trade if they choose. Parliament must change the law to protect them!"

William stroked his beard. "If we are going to take on something as big as this, we are going to need some good people on our team. Call W. T. Stead. He's the best news reporter in London, and better yet, he is a staunch supporter of our work. Get with him, and see what he suggests."

A week later W. T. Stead, Bramwell and his wife, Florence, and William and Catherine were all sitting around a large table in the "war room."

"And worse still, many of these girls are shipped overseas like cattle to work in foreign lands," W. T. said.

"How can that be?" Catherine asked. "Surely someone would notice and say something."

"Not the way they do it," W. T. continued. "It's appalling, but thousands of innocent girls, nearly all of them under sixteen, are kidnapped off the streets or sold by their parents or guardians. They are drugged and nailed into coffins that have air holes drilled in the bottom and are shipped to Brussels, Paris, and Antwerp."

"What a horror!" Florence exclaimed. "How awful it must be for those girls to wake up in a strange country, not knowing the language and having little hope of escape."

"Yes," W. T. replied, "I haven't unearthed any numbers yet, but I bet the suicide rate is very high."

"Small wonder," William agreed. "I have no doubt you've done your homework, W. T., but people are going to mock us for exaggerating a 'small' problem. Can we prove everything you say is true?"

W. T. nodded. "I have met with my old friend Detective Howard Vincent. He was the director of Scotland Yard's Criminal Investigation Department, and he confirmed all the facts I've found. But this is not what's going to convince people to take notice.

My reporter's instincts tell me we are going to have to put a girl as a plant in one of these institutions to expose the whole system. If it's written well, her story would cause a sensation. Even Parliament couldn't ignore it."

The group talked on through the morning until a plan was hatched. Bramwell and W. T. would find a poor family and "buy" one of their young daughters. Then they would sell the girl, rescue her before anything bad happened to her, and expose the whole sad practice of forcing young girls into a life of ruin.

To make sure the plan was legal, W. T. ran it past his lawyer, while William and Bramwell presented it to three powerful churchmen: the archbishop of Canterbury, the head of the Catholic Church in England, and the bishop of London. The bishop and the cardinal thought it was a grand scheme to expose evil, while the archbishop was less supportive because he believed that W. T. would be killed during the scheme.

Finally, on Tuesday, June 2, the plan went into action. A thirteen-year-old girl named Eliza Armstrong was bought from her mother for one pound. Then Bramwell and W. T. offered Eliza for sale, making sure she was "rescued" from the buyer before anything bad happened to her. Now W. T. had the face he needed to make the grim reality of London's worst trade come alive. He wrote a series of articles for the *Pall Mall Gazette* on the whole problem, and when the first article was published, it created an uproar. Many powerful men, including the queen's cousin and members of Parliament, secretly supported this terrible business, and they did not want any publicity of their secrets. The fate of the Salvation Army hung in the balance. Would thugs be allowed to harass it once again, or would the police continue to protect it, even when it exposed terrible things going on right under their noses?

The City of London sided with the powerful men and against the Salvation Army and the *Pall Mall Gazette.* W. T. Stead's articles were declared indecent, and policemen immediately arrested twelve paperboys for selling them. But others took up the challenge. Famous playwright George Bernard Shaw took many copies of the gazette and sold them on the Strand. By that evening every newspaper was sold out, and they were being resold on the black market for two and a half shillings apiece.

With the horrors of the trade now public knowledge in London, William Booth did everything he could to stir up enough indignation to change the law. He led huge rallies all over the country. Salvation Army officers everywhere collected signatures on a petition asking Parliament to raise the age of consent from thirteen years old to sixteen and give police the right to make inspections to see if any girls were being held captive.

Seventeen days later, nearly 400,000 signatures had been gathered. When the signatures were all glued onto a scroll, the scroll was over two and a half miles long! The people of England had spoken, but would the government hear them? William planned to make sure it did. He assembled a brass band and a legion of soldiers to accompany the petition to Parliament. They made such a fanfare that no one could claim the government had not noticed.

The public outcry forced the government to act, and on August 14, 1885, a bill was passed raising the age of consent from thirteen years old to sixteen and allowing police to perform inspections to look for girls who were held against their will.

A great victory had been won, although there was a price to pay for it. Some spiteful men, including the attorney general, had been greatly embarrassed by the scandal. They found a way to charge W. T. Stead and Bramwell Booth with kidnapping, and the two men stood trial. Bramwell was acquitted, but W. T. was sentenced to six months in Millbank Prison. He did not flinch as the punishment was read. He later told William that rescuing so many girls made it all worthwhile.

Australia soon followed with a similar law, as did many of the states in the United States. The Salvation Army had changed the first of many laws in favor of protecting the most vulnerable people in society.

All of this activity and publicity brought the Salvation Army into the national spotlight as never before.

Chapter 12

In Darkest England

Fifty-seven-year-old William Booth stepped onto New York's Cunard Pier on September 23, 1886. By now the Salvation Army boasted one hundred corps in North America manned by three hundred officers and over five thousand soldiers and cadets. William launched straight into a whirlwind tour that took him as far west as Kansas City. During the two-and-a-half-month visit, he spoke almost two hundred times, and nearly two hundred thousand Americans flocked to hear him.

By the time William climbed back aboard the ship for the trip home, he was exhausted. He was glad of the restful voyage across the Atlantic Ocean to England because there was much for him to do when he got home. The family was moving into a new house at Hadley Wood, and on February 8, 1887, daughter Kate was going to marry Arthur Clibborn, who served as her chief of staff. In what was to become a family tradition, they decided that instead of Kate changing her last name to Clibborn, both she and Arthur would change their names to Booth-Clibborn. William would perform the marriage ceremony for them.

After William's return to England, at about the time of the wedding, the Salvation Army "invaded" Germany, and William sent Ballington to take charge of the work in North America. Ballington was given the title "Marshal" to go with the new position.

Ballington and his wife, Maud, wrote many letters to William explaining what they were doing and why. One letter in particular touched William. It told how one of the New York officers had found a tiny, filthy baby dying in an otherwise empty tenement room. When the officer made inquiries about the whereabouts of the mother, he found that she had been on a five-day drinking spree and forgotten all about her baby. Ballington and Maud wrote that this spurred them to action.

As he read their letter, William remembered back to his early work in Nottingham, where he had seen mothers dose their babies with opium so that they could leave them alone all day. The mothers did not have the money to pay someone to look after their babies and needed to work for money to pay their rent. Even though the case in New York was a little different, it pointed to the need for someone to step in and take care of children whose mothers, for whatever reason, could not take care of them. And that is what the Salvation Army did in New York. It opened a daycare center for small children, and within weeks eight hundred cradles were rocking twenty-four hours a day.

Other news from America challenged William's thinking. The Salvation Army was working alongside the court system, so that when a prisoner from San Quentin was released, a Salvation Army officer was appointed as his probation officer. Sometimes the prisoners were also mandated to attend Salvation Army meetings for a week. "We see a need and we meet it," Ballington wrote, ending one of his letters.

This statement played on William's mind. Up until now he had believed in preaching the gospel anywhere and in any way possible. What he had not put much emphasis on was trying to change the social conditions of those they reached out to. But was it really the role of the Salvation Army to see a need—any need—and meet it? William answered that question for himself in the early hours of the cold, clear morning of December 1, 1887.

William was returning from Whitstable, in Kent, where he had been opening a new corps hall. As the carriage carrying him rattled across London Bridge, over the River Thames, William peered out into the dark. To his surprise he saw dozens of homeless men huddled in the nooks and crannies of the bridge and covered with scraps of newspaper to try to keep warm. But the newspaper was useless against the relentless cold, and the men shivered violently as they tried to keep their freezing fingers warm by blowing on them. Despite having spent most of his life working with people in the slums, William was shocked by the sight of these men, homeless and out in the open, and he decided something had to be done about it.

William diverted his carriage to Bramwell's house and dragged his son out of bed in the early hours of the morning. "Did you know that men sleep out in the open all night on the bridges?" he asked his bleary-eyed son.

"Well, yes. You mean you did not know?" Bramwell replied.

"You mean you knew, and yet you didn't do anything about it?" William snapped indignantly. "Well, go and do something! We have to do something. Rent a warehouse and warm it up. And find some blankets, and give those men a warm place to stay."

It was the beginning of a new facet of the work of the Salvation Army.

As William was working out what to do about the plight of the homeless, he received some devastating news. Catherine was diagnosed with breast cancer. Her Harley Street surgeon urged her to have an operation right away, but he conceded that even such a drastic step was unlikely to stop the cancer's progress.

While Catherine pondered the best treatment for her cancer, April 10, 1888, William's fifty-ninth birthday, rolled around. It was also the day that

Emma Booth married Fredrick Tucker. Fredrick had started the work of the Salvation Army in India. After the death of his first wife, he had returned to England to attend a conference about the future of the Salvation Army in India. While he was visiting the Booth family, he and Emma had fallen in love. And now they stood together at the altar exchanging marriage vows. For the wedding, to identify with the people of India, Fredrick dressed as a beggar. He wore a ragged turban and no shoes, and he symbolically placed a beggar's bowl on the altar. After the wedding the new Mr. and Mrs. Booth-Tucker planned to return to India and the work of the Salvation Army there.

At the wedding reception, William answered many questions about how the Salvation Army was helping the homeless through various social programs. Yet as he answered these questions, he was dissatisfied with what the army was doing.

"We have to do more," William told Bramwell as he paced the floor at Salvation Army headquarters. "We must find a way to demonstrate that God offers everyone a way out of poverty."

Bramwell nodded in agreement. "What we need is a coordinated effort to feed the poor—all of the poor. It's nearly impossible for a person to maintain a godly disposition when he is starving to death."

"I quite agree," William replied. "I'll talk to your mother about it, but I have an idea for cheap food depots. I know we have dabbled in soup kitchens, but this would be different. The depots would be set up all over England, and we would sell all sorts of different foods at wholesale prices in them. I think the West India Dock would be an ideal place to start. There's a lot of starving people down there."

"I agree," Bramwell said. "I'll get someone onto it right away."

"Commissary Flawn would be a good man to head it up," William said, thinking back to his old friend and one of his earliest converts in the East End. "He used to set up the chairs for my tent meetings, and he was in the food business. Talk to him and see what he has to suggest. Maybe there's more we can do than just offer food."

"Yes, General," replied William's dutiful son.

Within a month the cheap food depots were up and running, first at West India Dock and then at Clerkenwell and Marylebone. They sold potatoes and meat pies for threepence and two jam rolls for a penny. But the food depots were more than just food stalls. Each shop had a long dormitory attached to it where for fourpence a man could get hot water, soap, and a towel, as well as a good night's sleep in a warm hall.

The establishment of the food depots opened a floodgate of other innovative ideas on caring for the poor. William and Bramwell set up the first labor exchange in England at 36 Upper Thames Street, London, directly behind the Salvation Army's international headquarters. Men who needed a job could fill out an application listing their skills, and employers could come and find new employees. In the first two months it was open, two hundred unemployed men were matched to jobs.

While this was going on, William tried to support Catherine in any way he could. She had agreed to the surgery to treat her cancer, but recovery from the operation was a painful process, especially since she refused to use morphine to dull the pain. In fact, after the operation William watched sadly as Catherine grew weaker and weaker. Staff Captain Carr was assigned to change the dressing on Catherine's wound, which would take many months to completely heal. Before the wound had fully healed, however, William and Catherine received the news that the operation had not been successful. The cancer was continuing to spread.

Still, William knew that his wife was not one to miss an opportunity, and in her bedridden state, she wrote hundreds of letters of encouragement to officers all over the world. At first she wrote them in her own hand, but as her muscles became weak, she dictated them to Captain Carr.

Meanwhile William was becoming more restless than ever about his plans for social change in England. In 1889 ten thousand London dockworkers went on strike in the hope of a guaranteed wage of sixpence an hour and a five-day workweek. Most of the men on strike did not have enough money saved to feed their families for more than a few days, and the situation soon became desperate. William, who was in full sympathy with the dockworkers' plight, ordered the Salvation Army to supply nearly 200,000 cut-price meals.

The dock strike went on for a month, and out of it a dockworkers' union was formed. The union eventually persuaded the rich dock owners to give in to the demands of the men. The crisis passed, but the aid the Salvation Army gave to the workers seeking a decent living wage made the army the heroes of the working poor.

All of this happened just as William approached his sixtieth birthday, which was on April 10, 1889. The event was celebrated in grand style at the Salvation Army's Congress Hall. The celebration began with a parade, complete with brass bands, followed by a traditional English dinner of roast beef and mashed potatoes. William sat under an enormous banner in the hall that read, "God Bless Our General."

Although Catherine was too ill to join William at the dinner table, she insisted on coming along, and she sat in an adjoining room listening to the speeches. Somehow, toward the end of the evening, she summoned up the strength to make her way into the dining room and say a few words. As William listened to her speak, tears came to his eyes. He thought back on all that the Salvation Army had achieved, and he knew it would not have been possible without Catherine's steadying hand.

With his birthday celebration behind him, William decided to move Catherine to the ocean in the hope that it would be a restful environment for her. He left the day-to-day work in Ballington's hands and rented a small house in Clacton, on England's southeast coast.

William thought he needed a rest, too, but after a week at the small house, he was his usual restless self. Although the cheap food depots were functioning well, William grew frustrated at the idea that there was more he should be doing. Sitting beside the sea one day, puzzling over what to do, the idea of writing a book came to mind. This would be very different from anything he had written before. It would be a book about the evils of poverty in England and the extraordinary difficulties poor men and women encountered when they tried to better themselves.

The book idea energized William, and he rushed off a letter to W. T. Stead asking him to help him in the writing of the manuscript. In May 1889 W. T. and William met to plan out the book. They agreed that the first thing they needed to do was gather facts. Without them it would be impossible to stir people into action. A newly published book entitled *The Life and Labour of the People of London* and written by a man named Charles Booth proved a very helpful starting point. It contained many statistics on the poor in London, and William sent out a team of Salvation Army officers to gather still more facts. Several weeks later piles of surveys and statistics cluttered every available space in William's office.

As he read a report prepared by Frank Smith, William grew more and more convinced he was on the right track. The report described the circumstances of twelve men who had been found sleeping on the Embankment on the nights of June 13 and 14, 1890. William read the first story aloud to W. T.:

> No.1. "I've slept here two nights; I'm a confectioner by trade; I come from Dartford. I got turned off because I'm getting elderly. They can get young men cheaper, and I have the rheumatism so bad. I've earned nothing these two days; I thought I could get a job at Woolwich, so I walked there, but could get nothing. I found a bit of bread in the road wrapped up in a bit of newspaper. That did me for yesterday. I had a bit of bread and butter today. I'm 54 years old. When it's wet we stand about all night under the arches."

"Grim, isn't it?" William said to W. T. when he had finished reading. "But then, you know as much about this as I do. We have to find the best way to communicate this to the general public. So many of them are tucked up in bed by ten o'clock each night, and they have no idea there is a whole seething undermass of people outside their doors with nowhere to sleep. Listen to this—it's another man."

> No. 5. Sawyer by trade, machinery cut him out. Had a job, haymaking near Uxbridge. Had been in the same job lately for a month, got 2 shillings and 6 pence a day....

> Has been odd jobbing a long time, earned 2 pence today, bought a pen'orth of tea and ditto sugar but can't get any place to make the tea; was hoping to get to a lodging house where he could borrow a teapot, but had no money.

William shook his head. "They go on and on. We know there are thousands of such stories being played out every day in London. Here's a tailor who tried to sleep under cover in Covent Garden and got moved on by the police, and another man whose father was a clergyman. He was down on his luck after his employer went broke. And another man who minds horses and sells match boxes. He made threepence all day. And look, this report says, 'There are women who sleep out here. They are decent people, mostly charwomen and such like who can't get work.'"

"Yes, you're right," W. T. said. "There are hundreds of sad stories like these, and Charles Booth's book exposes many of them. Your book will have to be different. To be any use, it's going to have to offer solutions as well as outline the problems. Let's face it, most respectable people assume that the Poor Laws work well and that these people are too lazy to take advantage of them."

"Well, listen to this," William said as he continued scanning the paper in his hands. "'Earned nothing yesterday, slept at a casual ward; very poor place, get insufficient food, considering the labor.

Six ounces of bread and a pint of skilly for breakfast, one ounce of cheese and six or seven ounces of bread for dinner. Tea same as breakfast—no supper.'

"Now that's the real state of the Poor Laws. The law says that the state is legally responsible for providing food and shelter to every man, woman, or child who is utterly destitute. But how cruel the standard is. You can't claim you are destitute until you have nothing whatsoever to claim as your own. Piece by piece every stick of furniture must be sold, and any tools of your trade have to be sold or pawned as well. You can't even own a teapot. Only then will the state allow you to stay in a workhouse. And once you go into the workhouse, there's no way to get out.

"Or if you still have an ounce of self-respect and flicker of hope of finding a job, the only option is the casual ward. That soon becomes a nightmare, too. Under the existing regulations, if you go to a casual ward on a Monday, you have to stay inside the compound until Wednesday morning. In that time you have to either break half a ton of rocks a day or untwist four pounds of rope so that it can be used to caulk ships. Either job is grueling. Indeed, I'd like to challenge our readers to do that on an ounce of cheese and a couple of slices of bread a day. Besides, the worst complaint the men have is that they can't get out to look for a job, so they leave the casual ward no better off than when they arrived."

"I agree," W. T said. "Small wonder that there are only eleven hundred thirty-six beds in the casual wards for all of London, and many of those go empty. The authorities seem to go out of their way to make them the most unhelpful—not to mention unhealthy—places on earth. With these stories and others like them that your officers are collecting, I think we can offer both the facts of the matter and the feelings that go along with poverty. I mean, how many Englishmen know that 10 percent of the population lives in desperate poverty?"

"Good, we must get straight onto it then. I just wish I could think of a suitable name for the book, something that's eye-catching," William said.

A week later William opened a package from Bramwell. Inside was a newly published book written by Henry Morton Stanley, the explorer who had found David Livingstone in the interior of Africa. William started reading right away. The book opened with the story of Stanley and a group of guides from Zanzibar hacking their way through dense and seemingly impenetrable jungle half the size of France. Soon the men began to despair that there was any way through it, and as they met cannibals, slave traders, and disease along the way their gloom grew. It was a vivid picture of the obstacles that were reflected in the book's title, *In Darkest Africa.*

The more William thought about Stanley's book, the more comparisons he made to London. Weren't both places under a dense cloud causing men to despair? Malaria might claim lives in Africa, but what about London? Wasn't the River Thames nicknamed The Great Stink, with its 370 sewers spewing filth into the river between Westminster and London Bridge? In the summer the gooey black sludge was six feet thick all the way across, and it stunk so badly that the House of Commons library had to be closed. But what about all the poor people who lived along the banks of the river? They didn't have the luxury of fleeing from the foul smell. Surely the cholera epidemics in London were every bit as devastating as the malaria in Africa. And didn't some rich slumlords prey on their tenants as willingly as any slave trader dealt in human misery?

"Yes," William mumbled to himself, "we are captivated by human squalor and suffering on another continent, but we are not as willing to confront it at our very door. If Stanley can have his *In Darkest Africa,* then I shall write *In Darkest England!*"

Chapter 13

Echo Around the World

William's title was a hit with W.T., and the two men started work writing the book. William began with the introduction, making the comparison to Henry Stanley's book many times. It was not long before another book he read gave him more ideas on helping the poor. This book, entitled *Past and Present,* by Thomas Carlyle, had been written forty years before. William read one particular paragraph that captivated his imagination: "There are not many horses in England, able and willing to work, which have no due food and lodgings and go about sleek coated and satisfied in heart… the human brain, looking at these horses, refuses to believe in the same possibility for Englishmen."

William's mind whirled at these words. There wasn't a single person in London who would not understand the comparison between a horse's needs and the needs of a human being. Over a period of several days, William came up with the "Cab Horse's Charter." He rushed into Catherine's room to explain it to her. "Just think," he said, "if every person in England were entitled to the same care and consideration as a cab horse. That wouldn't be too much to ask, would it?"

"I suppose not," Catherine replied. "Tell me exactly what you are thinking."

"Well," William said, seating himself in a chair beside his wife's bed, "what it means is that in London when a weary, careless, or stupid cab horse falls down and blocks traffic, people do not stand around debating whether it should be helped back on its feet and whether it will fall again if they do. No, all necessary energy is spent on getting the animal up and the traffic flowing again. His load is taken off, his harness unbuckled or even cut. In fact, we do everything we can to help him on his way again."

"I see," Catherine said. "So you are saying that we should help the destitute before we stop to ask how they got in that condition. Get them moving, and then when they are clean and fed, find out how they got so low."

"Precisely, my dear. If we can do that for a London cab horse, why can't we do it for a person? But there's more." William stood up and paced the floor. He was too excited to sit down any longer.

"A London cab horse has three things: shelter for the night, food to eat, and work given to it so that it can earn its corn. And that's what I'm going to call the Cab Horse Charter in my book. When a man is down, he is helped up, and as long as he lives, he has the right to food, shelter, and work. What do you think?"

Catherine smiled at William and nodded.

William went on. "It is such a humble standard, but one that's unattainable by one tenth of our population. I'm going to call them the 'submerged tenth' because hardly anyone ever thinks about their needs and rights. That is a shame on all of us, much more of a shame than if we left fallen horses to die in the streets. But we would never do that!"

William sat down once again and held Catherine's hand. "My dear, I am so glad you are here to listen to my ideas. You have helped me shape so many of them. This book will go on as a legacy from both of us; I am sure of that. Positive, in fact."

It was Sunday morning, September 14, 1890, when W. T. made a triumphant announcement to William. "It's finally finished!" He tied a string around the pile of manuscript pages for I*n Darkest England and the Way Out*. "This work will echo around the world," he concluded, "and I will rejoice with exceeding joy when it does."

Catherine, who was lying on the couch, replied in a husky whisper, "And I will rejoice, too. Thank God."

"Yes, thank God indeed!" William replied. "It has been a long labor, but I am pleased with the result. It's one thing to explain how many destitute people there are in England, but adding 'The Way Out' section gives people ways to help the poor out of poverty. I have decided to donate the royalties from the book to my Darkest England fund, and I aim to raise a million pounds more for the fund to bring the schemes outlined in the book to life."

"That's a lot of money to raise and to spend, but if anyone can raise it, you can," W. T. said.

"Yes, it is a lot of money," William said, "but not so much if you compare it to other things. When King Theodore of Abyssinia captured two diplomats, the British government spent ten million pounds to rescue them. And the failed attempt to rescue General Gordon from Khartoum cost many more millions of pounds than that. If the British government spends such amounts of money to rescue a few people, why not raise and spend a million pounds rescuing the poor?"

"And think of the consequences if something is not done to help them," Catherine said. "I remember challenging the bishop of Carlisle many years ago. I said to him, 'My dear sir, the day is coming when these masses will require to be dealt with. Will it not be better to face them with the gospel than with the sword?' As I recall, he never gave me an answer."

"Quite right," William said. "In fact, I think I shall raise that point in my wedding sermon on Thursday."

"Ah, the wedding," Catherine sighed. "I'm so sorry that I will be too weak to go. Please give

Herbert and Cornelie my love. Set me a chair at the service and put my portrait on it so that I can be there in semblance if not in reality."

William nodded, too overcome to speak. He hated to leave Catherine and go to London for their son Herbert's wedding, but she insisted. And so he went, and at the service he did as she wished, placing an empty chair and her portrait at the front of the hall. As soon as the wedding was over, William raced back to Clacton to be at Catherine's side and tell her about the wedding and the latest news of the Salvation Army's work around the world.

Two weeks later, on October 1, Catherine suffered a massive hemorrhage. The family was summoned from all over England. Bramwell, Eva, Marian, and Lucy hurried to their mother's side. Herbert arrived later, having been away on his honeymoon. The other Booth children were all serving overseas and could not be there right away.

The children gathered around their mother's bed, alternately singing hymns and the old Salvation Army songs they had been reared on and praying. At night William asked to sit alone with Catherine, and the couple talked about the old times together. They reminisced about when Catherine interrupted William during the service back in Gateshead. It was many years ago now, but that incident had launched her preaching career. And they remembered mixing Christmas puddings with the children and boiling them in the copper in the laundry. They remembered the smiles that came to the faces of those who received the puddings. Those smiles alone had made it all worthwhile being out in the slums on Christmas morning. The Salvation Army still continued the practice, giving out thousands of puddings to the poor on Christmas day. These and so many other memories flooded back to William and Catherine.

On the night of October 3, as William sat beside her, Catherine slipped the wedding ring off her finger and pressed it into William's hand. Looking him in the eyes she said, "By this token we were united for time, and by it now we are united for eternity."

William bowed his head and let the tears fall onto the Salvation Army flag that was draped over Catherine's bed like a quilt. "You have all my love," he replied, "and you always will."

The following afternoon, Saturday, October 4, 1890, Catherine pointed to the framed text over her bed. Bramwell lifted it down and placed it on the bed so that she could read it. It said, "My grace is sufficient for you."

After she had read the text, Catherine beckoned each of the children to her side and kissed them. Finally it was William's turn. As he bent down and put his arms around his wife, she smiled one last time and died.

Early that evening George Railton arrived at the house and offered to take over the funeral arrangements. William gratefully took up his offer, and the next day a plain oak coffin with a glass cover arrived at the house. Catherine Booth's body was laid in the coffin, which was then draped with the Salvation Army flag and carried out to a wagon for the trip to London.

William accompanied his wife's body to London, where the "Army Mother" was laid in state at Clapton Congress Hall. Next to her coffin was placed the empty chair and portrait from Herbert's wedding. When he saw the chair and portrait, William recalled Catherine's words: "Set me a chair at the service and put my portrait on it so that I can be there in semblance if not in reality." Tenderly he bent over and kissed the portrait. He knew that Catherine, his wife of thirty-five years, would be with him every day for the rest of his life, her words of encouragement echoing in his mind as he pressed on.

Over the next five days more than fifty thousand mourners filed past Catherine's coffin. They came from every walk of life. Salvation Army captains walked next to chimney sweeps, and lawyers followed grooms and boot polishers.

On the morning of October 13, the coffin was taken from Clapton Congress Hall to Olympia Hall, where thirty-six thousand people had jammed inside for the funeral. The service was unlike any other funeral ever held in London. Flags flew, representing all of the countries where the Salvation Army now worked. White streamers fluttered from the stage, and in true Salvation Army style, everyone wore a white armband of victory, not the usual black band to symbolize mourning.

The crowd sat silently as George Railton reminded them all of the message Catherine sent to the Salvation Army's twenty-fifth anniversary celebration three months before. "My place is empty, but my heart is with you. You are my joy and crown. Your battles, suffering, and victories have been the chief interest of my life for these twenty-five years. They still are... I am dying under the Army flag, and it is yours to live and fight under. God is my salvation and refuge in the storm."

William sat through the service with his right hand in his pocket fingering Catherine's wedding ring.

Once the service was over, the coffin was placed in a hearse, and William climbed into an open carriage immediately behind it. As he stood in the carriage, he caught a glimpse of the immense crowd that had gathered to watch the funeral procession. Behind were three thousand Salvation Army officers standing at attention awaiting George's orders to accompany the hearse. Soon the great procession moved off. William stood ramrod straight in the carriage as he looked out over the throng that lined the streets. They had come to pay their last respects to the woman he had known and loved.

Herbert and Bramwell Booth rode on horses behind William, and William's five daughters, Kate, Emma, Marian, Eva, and Lucy, followed in a second carriage. The only child not at the funeral was Ballington, who had not been able to get there from North America in time.

The funeral procession took four hours to wind its way from Queen Victoria Street along the Thames Embankment to the Abney Park Cemetery. William did not allow himself to sit for one minute of the procession.

When they arrived at the cemetery, the people all arranged themselves in an orderly fashion, and several of the Booth children said a few words. Then William held up his hand. He had found the strength to speak. He began in a faltering voice to explain that whenever he and Catherine had been apart, as they often were, he had counted the days and hours until they could be together again. And now that she had been "promoted to Glory," he asked the crowd if he should spend the rest of his life in limbo waiting to rejoin his wife. He answered himself with a resounding no.

"What, then, is there left for me to do?" William continued. "My work is plainly to fill up the weeks, days, and hours and cheer my poor heart as I go along with the thought that when I have served my Christ and my generation according to the will of God—which I vow this afternoon I shall do with the last drop of my blood—then I trust that He will bid me to the skies as He bade her." William then bent down and gently kissed Catherine's coffin.

When William had finished speaking, a hymn that Herbert had written years before was struck up and Catherine Booth's coffin was lowered into the ground. George Railton said a few quiet words, then turned to the crowd and pronounced a benediction.

"God bless and comfort the bereaved ones! God keep us who are left to be faithful unto death! God bless the Salvation Army!"

A chorus of "Amen" echoed around the cemetery.

William was relieved to think that Catherine's two-and-a-half-year struggle was over. And even though he hated to admit it to anyone, he was weary himself and hoped to have a long rest before returning to the "battle line." However, this was not to be. Three days after the funeral, William found himself in the middle of a publicity storm. *In Darkest England and the Way Out* was finally published and hit the streets. The howls of protest started immediately. Some church leaders were kind enough to merely label William an impossible dreamer. Did he really expect to start an international missing persons bureau or a farming program for poor city dwellers? Others, like Thomas Huxley, a staunch proponent of Charles Darwin's theory of evolution, were more scathing. Although Huxley was five years older than William, he rallied to oppose William's plans with the energy of a man half his age. He wrote twelve brusque letters to the *London Times,* giving blow-by-blow accounts of why he found everything about William Booth and his Salvation Army detestable.

Huxley's letters stirred up an incredible amount of hatred from people in a city that had just rallied around as the Army Mother was buried. William could hardly believe the change of heart. The magazine *Punch* began mocking William, calling him "Field Marshal von Booth," and he was accused of being everything from a pious rogue to a hypocritical scoundrel.

William Booth's ideas gained supporters as well as detractors. Winston Churchill, the Undersecretary of State, vigorously agreed with William, and Cardinal Manning, the head of the Catholic Church in Britain, stated publicly that he thought the Salvation Army was doing just what Jesus and the apostles would have done had they encountered the poor of Victorian England. Charles Spurgeon, the famous Baptist evangelist, added his stamp of approval. He wrote, "Five thousand extra policemen could not fill [the Salvation Army's] place in the repression of crime and disorder."

All of this controversy sold more books, and by the end of the month, ninety thousand copies had been sold and William was the most famous author in England. It seemed as if everyone was talking about him. Regrettably, much of the talk was negative. Some called him a childish idealist, a socialist, and a dangerous man bent on destroying the class structure that made the British empire all that it was.

There were many times when Bramwell stormed into his father's office, newspaper in hand. "Look at this!" he would say, his face flushed and his palms sweaty. "This is the last straw. You really must do something to combat this awful gossip."

William always gave him the same answer. "Bramwell, fifty years from now it will matter very little indeed how these people treated us. It will matter a great deal how we dealt with the work of God."

Now that William had published his plan of action—the way out—it was time to put it into practice. "We shall start with the matchmaking industry," he declared.

This was not a random choice. In his investigations of London's underbelly, the matchmaking industry had often come up. William had discovered that four thousand people were employed in the city making matches and matchboxes. The conditions they worked under were as bad as anything found in the British empire's most "heathen" outpost. Whole families, mostly made up of widows and small children, worked in factories for sixteen hours a day, six days a week. The children never attended school. In fact, most of them were too tired at the end of the day to eat the slices of stale bread their mothers put in front of them.

As bad as the shift work was, William found something even worse—the matches themselves. To cut the prices to a bare minimum, the factory owners rejected red phosphorous match heads in favor of the cheaper yellow phosphorous. There was just one problem: The red chemicals were harmless, and the yellow ones, deadly. And it was a slow death. The yellow phosphorous attacked the worker's jaws, mimicking a bad toothache. There was one sure way to tell whether it was a toothache or "phossy jaw." All a worker had to do was to stand in a lighted room at night, then after a couple of minutes snuff out the light. If the worker did have phosphorous poisoning, the unfortunate person's jaw would glow white in the darkness. Often the person's hands and clothes would also glow with eerie luminescence. Once phossy jaw set in, the side of the victim's face turned green, then black, then it filled up with pockets of puss, rotting from the inside out. Unable to eat and in excruciating pain, the worker starved to death.

William got to work setting an example as to how a matchmaking factory should be run. He drew up plans for a spacious and well-lit factory that would employ 120 workers. Donations started to arrive as sympathetic people read his book, and by May 1891 enough money had come in to get the factory up and running. He called the matches *Lights in Darkest England,* and of course no yellow phosphorous was ever used.

Within a year the factory was turning out more than a million boxes of matches. Better still, many members of Parliament and newspaper reporters toured the facility. As they did so, seeds were planted that would eventually lead to laws governing conditions in the workplace.

By the end of the year, *In Darkest England and the Way Out* had sold over 200,000 copies. All over England citizens continued to be at first scandalized by the revelations in the book and then drawn into debates about William Booth's "way out." Many were moved to give money, and the million pounds William planned to raise to help the poor swiftly flowed in.

Emboldened by the success of the match factory, William and the Salvation Army set about putting into practice a whole range of solutions he had outlined in the book. Work programs for the unemployed were started, and soon men were providing firewood for English hearths and making shaving mugs and tea caddies and cutlery with the Salvation Army's Blood and Fire crest on it. Others made clothing to sell, and in Essex, by the Thames estuary, a farm colony was established. Here 260 men farmed three thousand acres of land. They raised stock, grew vegetables, and tended a kiln that turned out two million bricks a year.

Other countries were experimenting with William's ideas, many of which the government of the state of Victoria in Australia implemented. And in Europe city officials donated buildings in the poorest slums to the Salvation Army with the mandate to house the unemployed and create work for them. The unofficial Salvation Army slogan became "Soup, Soap, and Salvation!" and much to William's delight, their work continued to grow.

Chapter 14

Everything the Salvation Army Was About

After a year of turmoil and mourning, William Booth was ready for a new challenge. He wrote to a friend, "It is a curious piece of comfort that anything is better than stagnation and being left alone."

William did not intend to be left alone. Ten thousand Salvation Army officers were now serving in twenty-six countries, and he intended to visit them all with encouraging words and evangelistic rallies. As 1891 rolled on, he handed over the daily running of the Salvation Army to Chief of Staff Bramwell, whom he had chosen years ago to become his successor. One of William's last orders before he left was to recall Emma Booth-Tucker from India, where she had become very ill living among the lowest Indian caste. He sent twenty-three-year-old Lucy to India to replace her. Lucy had a respiratory disease, and the doctor recommended a warmer climate to help her breathing.

William chose America as his first port of call, and on July 25, 1891, he set sail from Southampton. Just as he had on his previous visit, William pushed himself at a punishing pace. He returned to England, and then it was off to Germany for a whirlwind tour. Seventy-two-year-old William Booth had never allowed ill health to stop him from preaching, and now he refused to allow age to do that either. Over the next four years, he continued to hold mass rallies around Europe and England.

In 1894 Lucy married a Swedish officer she had met in India. Like the rest of William's sons-in-law, Lucy's husband continued the tradition of adding Booth to his name, becoming Emmanuel Booth-Hellborg. After their wedding the couple returned to India to continue their harrowing work there, and in 1895 William went to visit them.

It was his first trip to Asia, and William was particularly impressed with the Salvation Army workers in India. Their work among one very violent group aptly called the "Crims" reminded him of the early days when Hallelujah Lassies with tambourines had faced down Skeleton Army thugs.

The Crims were a lawless lot. They did not believe in washing, and when their clothes wore out, they simply stole new ones to replace their rags. In fact, stealing occupied much of their time. It was said that thieving was so inbred in them that when

Crim parents gave birth, the new baby's name was registered straightaway in the police register of felons. The Crims were also brutal with each other. If a man was arrested and put in jail, his wife would take a new husband. When the old husband was released from jail, a fight to the death with the new husband would follow. For the Crims heaven was a place where there were no police stations and where they could gamble all day long. When a Crim man died, a tiny wedge of gold was placed in his mouth at the funeral so that he would have money to place his first bet in the afterlife.

The Crims also had a reputation for being uncontrollable. When they were put in jail for their crimes, they simply kept escaping, and outside of jail they had nothing but contempt for the police and the rule of law.

The government had become so frustrated with the Crims that several years before, Sir John Hewett, lieutenant governor of the United Provinces, challenged the fledgling Salvation Army corps in India to work with these people. The Salvation Army accepted the challenge and established a village where Crims could live and work. Indeed, the government compelled many of them to live in the Salvation Army's village. On one occasion fifty Crims were brought to the village to live. The men were roped together, and because of their reputation for making trouble and escaping, 140 heavily armed policemen accompanied them. They released the fifty men into the custody of the five Salvation

Army officers overseeing the village, who already had 250 other incorrigible Crims to watch over.

At first it was slow going. The Crims could see no reason why they should change their lifestyle. They argued, why work when you can steal? Still the Salvation Army officers were equally determined to proclaim the gospel to them and see their lives and the lives of their families and friends changed. Over time it began to dawn on the Crims that the Salvation Army officers were not like the police or the government, who simply wanted to control them and keep them away from the rest of society. Salvation Army officers cared about what happened to them. They took time to be with them, talk to them, and understand them. As a result trust was slowly built. The Crims began opening themselves to the message the officers had to give and began taking their advice. Work schemes started to spring up, and before long many of the men and women were making hessian bags for, of all places, the local government treasury.

By the time William arrived to observe the work of the Salvation Army among the Crims, they had become hardworking, self-reliant people. Indeed, William found it hard to believe they were the same notorious people he had heard so much about. At a church meeting he watched as Crims took turns reading verses from the Bible and praying fervently for the conversion of their family and friends. One old Crim woman came up to William and confided, "To think of God as One instead of millions of gods and spirits is so restful."

A smile of satisfaction spread across William's face. Restfulness, yes. He had seen that same restfulness in the lives of other poor and downtrodden people in England and America as they had embraced the gospel and allowed God to change their lives. And that, after all, was what the Salvation Army was all about.

While William was overseas, Bramwell did something drastic that eventually split the Booth family in two. As chief of staff he had the right to move officers anywhere in the world, and he chose William's absence as a time to reshuffle several top-ranking Army officers—his brothers and sisters. Without any warning or consultation, he ordered Herbert in Canada to take command of the Salvation Army in Australia, while Eva, who served in London, was ordered to take command in Canada. Meanwhile Kate and Arthur Booth-Clibborn were moved from France to Holland, and Lucy and Emmanuel Booth-Hellborg were brought back from India to take over Kate and Arthur's old command. Ballington and Maud Booth were ordered to return to England from the United States, where they would trade posts with Emma and Frederick Booth-Tucker, who were serving as joint foreign secretaries of the Salvation Army.

In one day Bramwell created chaos in what his siblings rudely called "Bramwell's game of musical chairs." Letters and telegrams of complaint flew across the ocean to reach William in India.

Most of the resentment came because Bramwell had not consulted any of his brothers and sisters before issuing his orders. While they were used to taking orders from their father, none of the Booth children took well to obeying their brother, especially since he appeared to be high-handedly disrupting their lives and their work.

William understood how they felt. Kate, who wrote passionately, reminded him that she had served in France for ten years, starting two hundred stations and commissioning four hundred officers. Kate spoke French more fluently than English and had raised her seven children to think of themselves as French. She wanted to know what could possibly be achieved by removing her and Arthur from their post and replacing them with Lucy and Emmanuel, who had absolutely no experience in France.

Ballington was extremely angry about the challenge to his authority. He wrote to say that the people of New York were planning a mass protest rally at the thought of losing him. Even the mayor of the city promised to be on the platform at the rally.

Before all else, the Salvation Army was just that, an army, and success in an army depends on every soldier obeying his or her commanding officer. Bramwell was the chief of staff, and he had issued orders that were well within his jurisdiction, and so William would back them up. William saw himself as a general first and a father second. There was no way he was about to interfere and give his own children the right to disobey a command. He wrote to them, "The Salvation Army does not belong to the Booth family. It belongs to the Salvation Army.

So long as the Booth family are good Salvationists and worthy of commands, they shall have them, but only if they are. I am not the 'General' of a family, I am the General of the Salvation Army."

Once he had declared his support of Bramwell, William could only wait and see what his children would choose. Would they put their own personal feelings over their duty or not?

Meanwhile William continued on to Japan, where the Salvation Army had recently begun working. One of the main focuses for the army there was the thousands of girls imprisoned in the Yoshiwara, a square-mile walled city just one mile from the heart of Tokyo. Most of the girls who worked in the horrible trade of the three-centuries-old Yoshiwara did so because their parents had sold them to the owners of the evil businesses there to raise money for food or other family needs that arose during hard times. Technically the girls weren't sold; rather, a loan was made to a girl's parents, and when the loan was repaid, the girl would be free to leave. In practice this was not what happened. The interest rates were so high that the loans were never paid back, and the girls became the property of the business owners.

This terrible situation greatly concerned the Salvation Army officers in Japan, and they decided to do something about it. In researching the problem, they discovered that the buying and selling of girls had been outlawed in 1872. However, the law was written in such archaic language that few people understood it. The Salvation Army wrote out in plain language what the law said and what it meant to the girls trapped in the Yoshiwara. It published its explanation of the law in the *Toki-no-Koe,* the Japanese version of *The War Cry,* under the heading "An Open Letter to the Women in Licensed Quarters."

Early one morning fifty Salvation Army officers gathered in a hall to pray before setting out to distribute copies of *Toki-no-Koe* in the Yoshiwara. To the surprise of the owners of the shameful businesses, they marched right into the center of the complex and began distributing the magazine. Many of the girls appeared at the windows of the buildings and accepted copies of *Toki-no-Koe.* Several of the Japanese officers announced to the girls that any of them who wanted to escape would be welcome at the Salvation Army's rescue home, which they had just opened. "Why not come right now—today!" they added emphatically.

Suddenly the Salvation Army officers were under attack. Around three hundred stick-wielding thugs and bullies came charging down the street after them. The thugs surrounded the officers and began to beat them savagely. Finally a contingent of police arrived, chased off the thugs, and escorted members of the Salvation Army to safety. The officers were bloodied but unbowed. When newspaper reporters heard of the attack, they descended on Salvation Army headquarters, where officers vowed publicly that they would keep up the fight to end the illegal enslavement of girls. This declaration in turn led to one Salvation Army officer being taken prisoner, after which he was beaten and tortured by the owners of the disreputable businesses and their enforcers. Still the Salvation Army would not give up the fight. As one Western reporter stated, "There is no place where the Salvation Army women fear to enter, nor are the men less courageous."

Almost every newspaper in Japan backed the Salvation Army's stand with banner headlines such as "March on, Salvation Army, and Bring Liberty to the Captives." Such declarations got the attention of the Japanese people, who began to clamor for change. Eventually, after nearly a year of public outcry and the unrelenting efforts of the Salvation Army to rescue girls from the Yoshiwara, the Japanese government passed a new law. The law mandated that any enslaved girl who wished to receive her freedom could do so simply by going to the local police station and declaring her desire to be set free from her owner. Within two years of the beginning of the Salvation Army's efforts, thousands of girls had sought their freedom, and business in the Yoshiwara was less than half what it had been. The army had won an important battle! As in India, William reveled in all that was being done by the Salvation Army in Japan.

When William returned to England, some good news was waiting for him. Oxford University had awarded him an honorary doctorate of civil laws. As he was handed his diploma, William smiled to himself. Here he was, a man who had left school at age thirteen to become a pawnbroker's apprentice being awarded a degree from such a prestigious university. He just wished Catherine could have been there to experience the moment with him.

Meanwhile, the controversy that Bramwell had created hung like a black cloud over William. One year after the orders were issued, the worst possible outcome occurred. Ballington and Maud Booth formally resigned from the Salvation Army. One-third of the army's officers in America followed their lead and handed in their commissions. They then swore allegiance to an all-American counterpart that Ballington had founded. It was called the Volunteer Army, and in just about every way it mimicked the Salvation Army, with flags and uniforms and homeless shelters. There was, however, one major difference. The Volunteer Army was to be democratically run, with a five-yearly election to determine the next general. Ballington Booth won the vote for the first general, and so the Booth family now had two armies and two generals.

William was horrified by this move. In his eyes Ballington and Maud were defectors—traitors not only to the army they had sworn to serve but also to William personally. And now that they were not in the Salvation Army, he had no time for them. Over the years since he had become general, William had come to view every relationship, every moment of his day, in light of how it affected his army. In choosing to found the Volunteer Army, Ballington had cut himself off from his family.

Worse still, William had an idea that such defections would not stop with Ballington. Kate and Herbert were having a difficult time adjusting to their new postings, and he fretted that they too might leave the army.

Still the work went on. In December 1896 William was invited to visit British Prime Minister William Gladstone at Hawarden Castle in North Wales. Gladstone had read William's book, and the two men passed a pleasant afternoon discussing the ideas expounded in it.

In February of the following year, William met with the political leaders of the United States as well. He had the honor of opening the Senate with prayer and spending half an hour with President William McKinley. The president was eager to know William's impressions of Japan and the Far East and also to hear of the Salvation Army's work in America.

While William was in North America, he spent time with Emma and Fredrick and kept in close contact with Eva, who was off on her own adventure. Eva and seven other Salvation Army officers had gone to the Yukon Territory in Canada to share the gospel with the miners swept up in the Klondike gold rush. To get to the men they had paddled upriver for thirty-five days in freezing cold weather. Finally they arrived at Dawson City and set to work. It was a rough-and-tumble place and definitely a man's world. Eva wrote to her father, telling him that despite the hardships they were making good progress. Men were becoming Christians and attending church on Sunday, and many down-on-their-luck miners were being served hot cocoa or a meal and given a warm bed to sleep in.

William was proud of his daughter. Eva exemplified everything the Salvation Army was about. She was devoted, selfless, and fearless. Wherever there were people who needed to hear the gospel preached or to have the hand of Christian charity extended to them, she was willing to go, no matter what hardships she encountered along the way. William had seen that same spirit over and over again as he had traveled the world visiting Salvation Army corps. And as far as he was concerned, things were only just beginning. The old century was winding down, and a new one would dawn filled with more opportunities than ever for the Salvation Army to wage its battle around the world.

Chapter 15

Promoted to Glory

A new century dawned filled with hope and promise. William, who was an old, gray-bearded man of seventy, kept up his punishing schedule. On a trip to Norway, he was delighted to learn that the Salvation Army there was about to launch a fifty-foot lifeboat named the *Catherine Booth*. The idea for a lifeboat had been advanced several years before by a Norwegian Salvation Army officer named Emil Ovsen, but the real need for it was brought to the public's attention in October 1899, when a frigid storm swept through the cod-fishing grounds. When it had abated, the sea was strewn with the wreckage of twenty-nine vessels and 140 fishermen had perished.

The *Catherine Booth* was built to a radical new design. The vessel had airtight compartments so that even if she were hit or swamped, she would not sink or capsize. She was also equipped with the latest innovations, such as a cannon that fired flares and drums of oil to calm the waves while fishermen were transferred from their sinking vessel to the lifeboat.

William seldom allowed himself to slow down. Ever punctual, he began his day at 6 A.M. with one hour of paperwork and letter writing before eating his spartan breakfast of dried toast and hot tea. He never napped and took every opportunity to keep working. On train trips he converted his carriage into an office on rails. While his secretary sat on the floor with the typewriter on the seat, William would dictate letters to him for three or four hours straight.

Although the general had no intention of slowing down, three events over the next two years left him feeling weary and alone. In January 1902 Kate made the announcement that she and her husband Arthur Booth-Clibborn were resigning from the Salvation Army. Even though William had thought this might happen, it was still a terrible shock to him. Of all his children, Kate was the one most like him—strong-willed, talented, and stubborn. In turn, Kate's resignation stirred up Herbert and Cornelie Booth's frustration, and by May their resignations were also sitting on William's desk. This left Bramwell, Emma, Marian, Eva, and Lucy loyal to the Salvation Army and, in William's strict interpretation of things, loyal to him as father.

In 1903 there were no more resignations, but tragedy struck the family in another way. In October Emma Booth-Tucker, commander in chief of the Salvation Army in the United States, was traveling by train when her carriage derailed and hit a water tower. Forty-three-year-old Emma was the only passenger killed. She left behind a distraught husband and six young children. Eva took over as national commander of America, and Fredrick made plans to return to London with the children.

The news clippings of the funeral reached William in London. The *New York Daily News* reported, "It is said that the funeral was the largest held in the city for a woman, and that the crowd which followed her to her grave was the largest which ever attended any public funeral except that of General Grant."

With the newspaper clippings were a handwritten note from Eva and a short prayer written by Motee, Emma's twelve-year-old daughter. Motee had read the prayer at her mother's grave:

> O Lord, we thank Thee that our mother died upon the battlefield. She did not die at home. But there upon the prairie she left her sword. O Lord, don't allow us to let it lie there, but help us to pick it up and go forward, so that when we die, You may say to us, "Well done!" Don't let us live so that you will have to say we have just done ordinarily, or middling, but let us live so that you will

> say, "Well done! You have done the best that could be done!"—as you said to our precious Mama.

"That granddaughter of mine is cast in the family mould," William mused to himself after he read the prayer. Then quietly he shut the door to his office, laid his head on his desk, and wept.

Still, an old soldier must press on, and that is just what William Booth did. In June of the following year, he was invited to Buckingham Palace for an audience with King Edward VII. The king commended William on the work of the Salvation Army and the role it played in improving the lives of countless British citizens. Before William left, the king asked for his autograph. William wrote:

> Your Majesty,
> Some men's ambition is art,
> Some men's ambition is fame,
> Some men's ambition is gold,
> My ambition is the souls of men.

As William's work of winning the souls of men continued, it did so in a modern way. It was the dawn of the automobile, and William quickly realized that if he traveled in one of these new contraptions, he could visit many of the smaller towns and villages that were not readily accessible by train. He assigned Bramwell to work out the details, and on August 9, 1904, William set out with a motorcade of six cars to reach people along the highways and byways of England. William rode in an open Napier touring car with red wheels. Accompanying him on the trip were his old friends and fellow soldiers, George Railton and Elijah Cadman.

Riding in a motorcar could be a harrowing experience. The roads were narrow, rutted, and dusty. And when it rained, they could quickly turn into a sea of mud that could bog a car down to its axles. And the horses that shared the roads did not take kindly to automobiles. It was not uncommon for them to rear and bolt when a car approached. Yet all of these inconveniences did not deter seventy-five-year-old William Booth. Rather they energized him! A month later he had traveled a bone-jarring 1,224 miles and addressed 164 meetings. Some of these meetings were small affairs held outside butcher shops in tiny villages, while others were huge and attended by lords and mayors alike. Some of William's favorite stopovers were factories, where the owners would often stop the machines to allow everyone to hear him speak. Once, on the street outside their factory, seven hundred hardened workmen knelt as William led them in a simple prayer.

In the spring of 1905, William was off again, this time to inspect Salvation Army outposts in Australia and New Zealand. En route he visited the Holy Land to fulfill a lifelong dream. On March 9, 1905, William knelt in the Garden of Gethsemane, where under the shade of an ancient olive tree, he fervently prayed for God to bless the world. When he rose, he paused to speak to a leper and kiss his hand. From there he toured Solomon's temple and the tomb of Lazarus at Bethany. He also carried the Salvation Army flag up Mount Calvary and then led the Salvationists with him in reciting the last verse of the hymn "When I Survey the Wondrous Cross."

Upon his return from New Zealand and Australia, William received another honor. On October 26, 1905, William, accompanied by Bramwell and a thousand officers, marched through the crowded streets of London from the Salvation Army's international headquarters to the Guildhall. The city fathers had wanted to send a lavish coach for William to ride in, but William had refused, choosing instead to walk like a common man.

At the Guildhall William was handed a small oak casket. The city fathers had wanted it to be a gold casket, but William had rejected the idea, calling such a casket a waste. Inside the oak casket was a sheet of parchment conferring on William the Freedom of the City of London. Also inside the casket were one hundred guineas, the amount of money the city would have spent on the gold casket.

In his speech at the ceremony, Sir Joseph Dimsdale, the city chamberlain, talked of the "imperishable monuments" William had erected. "These," he said, "speak of a divine ambition and a zeal the boldest patriot might be proud to feel. We are glad to pay the highest tribute which can be rendered by us and accepted by him, namely the regard of the City of London—and through the city, our country—expressed in our offer of the Freedom of a City which has ever striven for religious liberty; and a city which has benefited incalculably by General Booth's exertions."

After the ceremony William trudged back to Salvation Army headquarters, where he promptly placed the one hundred guineas in the social fund.

Not to be outdone by London, Nottingham, the city of William's birth, decided it was time to honor him. City fathers there conferred on him the Freedom of the City.

William made another tour to the United States in 1907. He listened with great pride as Commander Eva Booth told him about how Salvation Army soldiers had toiled in the aftermath of the San Francisco earthquake. Many people lost everything in the tragedy, and the army had rallied round to provide food, shelter, and comfort to people.

It was on his sixth motor tour of Great Britain that William finally met an enemy he could not face down. He had traveled fifteen hundred miles in five weeks. Then in Monmouthshire he was crippled over with pain in his right eye. Soon William could not see, and reluctantly he called a halt to the tour and returned to London to see a specialist. The doctor gave William some hopeful news. He had cataracts in both eyes, but they could be operated on.

The surgery on William's eyes was carried out just before Christmas 1908, and it appeared the operation had been a complete success. Early in the new year William was back on the road in his motorcade.

Sadly, the scar in his left eye did not heal properly, and William quickly found himself blind in one eye. He returned to London, where his doctor ordered him to rest. But no one was going to give General William Booth orders! He continued his busy schedule, embarking on a visit to Europe.

In Sweden he had an audience with King Gustav, and in Norway he met with King Haakon. In Norway William was also gratified to learn that his wife's namesake, the lifeboat *Catherine Booth,* had been put to excellent use. During the cod fishing season of February and March, it plied the waters around the Lofoten Islands. So far it had rescued sixteen hundred boats, towing them to the safety of the majestic fjords. About forty-five hundred fishermen had been saved during those rescues. The *Catherine Booth* spent the remainder of the year ferrying Salvation Army officers to remote fishing villages. As a result of the lifesaving work the *Catherine Booth* did, the officers received a warm welcome and preached to attentive ears.

At first William managed to get along quite well with sight in only one eye, but as the sight in his right eye began to deteriorate, he faced many new challenges. It became increasingly difficult for him to see the edges of the platform when he spoke, and those around him were concerned that he might walk right over the edge. To help prevent this, his secretary would outline the stage in large quantities of white ribbon, the color that William found easiest to distinguish. Even when he could no longer see his audience, William held them spellbound, from the humblest housecleaner to the kings and princes who came to hear him speak.

William insisted that all the news that came into Salvation Army headquarters from around the world be read aloud to him. He wanted to know what was happening in every area of his command so that he could pray and dictate notes of encouragement. He smiled when he heard of Eva's latest idea. She had declared Thanksgiving Day 1909 "Boozer's Day." On this day the Salvation Army in New York City mounted an all-out campaign to alert citizens to the horror of alcoholism and bring hope to the alcoholics themselves. They achieved this in a style that William himself would have been pleased to invent. Since there was no public bus service on Thanksgiving Day, Eva was able to hire the green double-decker buses that normally drove up and down Fifth Avenue. Members of the Salvation Army manned the buses, along with a large wagon from the city water department. Young girls banged tambourines and men blew tubas as they made their way. When they encountered a pub, a number of the Salvation Army officers would leap from the buses to "invade" the drinking establishment, where they begged, pleaded with, and cajoled drunks to board the buses and the wagon and go to the army's memorial hall with them.

People watched in amazement as the unusual procession made its way, led by a giant papier-mâché whiskey bottle with a man chained to it.

Men moved along beside the buses and wagon to make sure none of the twelve hundred drunks on board fell off or tried to run away. At the Salvation Army hall the bewildered drunks stumbled inside to be served strong, black coffee and donuts.

Inside the hall the atmosphere was soon ripe with the smell of unwashed bodies and alcohol. Many of the reporters who had rushed to the scene were barely able to stay in the room, but members of the Salvation Army, who overlooked the stench, moved compassionately among the drunks. After the men had sobered up some, they were issued a challenge. Who would invite God to help them change their ways? Two hundred men surged forward and knelt at the penitent form. Some of them were destined to rank among the Salvation Army's best soldiers.

In a letter to her father, Eva relayed how the parade had caused a firestorm of publicity. For the first time many men in city government had become aware of the vast numbers of drunks in the city and the need to help them find a way out of their predicament. William sent a telegram to Eva with just two words in it: "Fully approve."

By early 1912 William's doctor convinced him to have another eye operation. Before he went into the hospital, William spoke to seven thousand Salvation Army officers at London's Albert Hall. While physically frail, his voice carried to the back of the hall as he delivered what was to be the last of over sixty thousand sermons he had preached in his life. In the process of delivering all those sermons, he had crisscrossed the world many times, covering over five million miles.

William's final sermon was as short and easy to understand as always, and it hammered the same themes he had faithfully preached on throughout his life. He ended the sermon by saying, "While women weep as they do now, I'll fight; while little children go hungry as they do now, I'll fight; while men go to prison, in and out, in and out, I'll fight; while there yet remains one dark soul without the light of God, I'll fight—I'll fight to the very end!"

It was the rallying cry of an old general, and it was dutifully recorded and sent to the sixteen thousand Salvation Army officers then serving in fifty-eight countries around the world. When he was done, William waved a farewell to those gathered in Albert Hall and quipped, "I am going into dry dock for repairs."

But the repairs failed to restore William's sight, and by his eighty-third birthday, he had to face the reality that he would never see again. It was a sad month for William, and it was made sadder when Bramwell broke some stunning news to his father. The "unsinkable ship," the RMS *Titanic,* had struck an iceberg in the North Atlantic and sunk within minutes. Her sinking cost the lives of some fifteen hundred men, women, and children. One of those who perished on the ship was William's old friend W. T. Stead, who had been jailed for his part in changing Britain's laws to protect girls like Annie

Swan and who had faithfully helped William write *In Darkest England and the Way Out.* Several officers in the Salvation Army were also lost in the sinking of the ship.

When he had recovered from the initial shock, William dictated a telegram to President William Taft in the United States.

> My heart is moved by the fearful calamity which has befallen the world in the loss of the *Titanic*—moved with sorrow for the dead, among whom are some of my long-tried friends; moved with sympathy for the living, whose loss can never be repaired, and moved in its deepest sources of feeling concerning that sudden and awful summons into the presence of God.

William paused to wipe the tears from his eyes before he went on.

> I pray that it may speak to the multitudes of the reality and nearness of the world to come, and the urgency and overwhelming necessity of preparing for it. God bless and comfort you all!

By mid-August, William himself was coming close to the "reality and nearness of the world to come." He began drifting in and out of consciousness, barely aware of what was going on around him. The Blood and Fire flag he had carried up Mount

Calvary was draped over his bed. His officers and soldiers watched as the life ebbed from William Booth's eighty-three-year-old body. On August 20, 1912, Bramwell, Florence, Marian, and Lucy gathered around his bed. A doctor stood nearby. At 9 P.M. William's breathing grew irregular and then faltered and stopped.

"Is this death?" Bramwell asked the doctor.

Dr. Milne took William's hand and felt for a pulse. Then he reached over and closed William's unseeing eyes. "This is death," he replied quietly.

"Now he is with our mother," Bramwell said. He picked up a telegram that was on the nightstand. It was from Eva, and it read, "Kiss him for me." Bramwell Booth placed the telegram in his father's hand and bent and kissed him one last time before walking sadly out of the room. He had arrangements to make. His father had been "promoted to glory," and he deserved one last salute—a fitting funeral.

At midnight a motor hearse transported William's coffin to Clapton Congress Hall. Word of William's death had already spread like wildfire throughout London. As the hearse made its way to the hall, a row of cars filled with reporters and photographers formed in line behind it. The motorcade drove slowly through the winding streets. At each police station it passed along the route, all of the lights were turned on, and rows of detectives, inspectors, and constables stood bareheaded in a silent tribute to the general who had commanded a worldwide army.

By the next morning a banner hung in the front window of the international headquarters of the Salvation Army. It read, "The General Has Laid Down His Sword." William had held the post for fifty-three years.

William's body lay in state for three days, during which time more than 150,000 people from every walk of life came to pay their last respects. Over a dozen heads of state sent wreaths, and messages of sympathy addressed to Bramwell Booth arrived from leading men and women all over the world. King George wrote, "Only in the future shall we realize the good wrought by him for his fellow creatures. Today there is universal mourning for him. I join in it."

American President William Taft sent a message that said, "In the death of your good father the world loses one of its most effective practical philosophers."

Even the newspapers, which had once written so scathingly about William and ridiculed him as "General von Booth," could not now find enough words with which to praise him. The editor of the *Daily Telegraph* stated enthusiastically, "Whatever we may think of William Booth, and of the wonderful organization which he so triumphantly established, it is certain that he belonged to the company of saints.... We judge him to be one of the chief and most serviceable figures of the Victorian age."

As expected, William's funeral service was huge. On Tuesday, August 27, 1912, people lined up for hours outside Olympia Hall, waiting for the service to begin. Only the first forty thousand people could be seated. Those who were fortunate enough to get inside found themselves sitting in a huge hall decked out for the occasion with flags and white streamers, just as it had been decorated twenty-two years before for Catherine Booth's funeral.

Accompanied by ten thousand uniformed members of the Salvation Army marching in lockstep and forty bands, the hearse bearing General William Booth's body drove slowly along from Olympia Hall after the service. The heart of London came to a standstill for four hours as the long procession wound its way through the densely crowded streets. Three thousand policemen were on duty to control the crowd, but few were needed to keep the peace. As the hearse passed, mourners stood in silence.

Finally the hearse drove through the gates of Abney Park Cemetery, where William was laid in a grave beside Catherine. His tombstone read:

William Booth
Founder & 1st General Of The Salvation Army
Born 1829
Born Again In The Spirit 1845
Founded the Salvation Army 1865
Went To Heaven 20th August 1912

Bramwell, Marian, Eva, and Lucy, of course, all attended their father's funeral. But Kate and Herbert were also there, even though they had been estranged from William, and Ballington, still living in the United States, sent a letter of condolence.

When William's will was finally read, everything he owned amounted to less than five hundred pounds. The man who had raised millions of pounds for his army had lived out his life in frugal simplicity.

For weeks after William was buried, the rumor spread that Queen Alexandra had come to the funeral in disguise. No one could prove whether the rumor was true or not, but in one sense it did not matter. What mattered was that no one thought it strange or unbelievable that a queen might have been standing shoulder to shoulder with a charwoman at William Booth's funeral.

Chapter 16

Stringing Lights Around the World

It was 1935 and General Evangeline Booth, the fourth general of the Salvation Army, stood on an old railway platform seeking shelter from the rain as she waited for her driver to repair the broken-down car. A small crowd gathered around her, but Eva was too tired and wet to talk with them. Besides, her voice was hoarse from the preaching she had done that evening.

As she stood peering into the darkness, a policeman strolled over and climbed the platform steps. He tipped his hat at Eva and said, "Begging your pardon, General, but there's a man down there who says he must talk to you."

Eva sighed. "Then let him come up," she replied.

"But he can't," the policeman said.

"Why not?" Eva asked.

"Because he can't climb the stairs."

"And why can't he climb the stairs?"

"Because he's ninety-three years old, ma'am."

"Ninety-three years old!" Eva responded, wondering what the old man could possibly want to talk to her about.

"He says he has come two hundred miles to see you," the policeman added.

"That can't be!" Eva replied.

"He really does want to see you," the police officer said apologetically.

"If he's come all that way, I suppose I had better see what he wants." With that she pulled her jacket tight around her and descended the stairs from the platform.

Soon she was standing in front of an aged man. His back was bent in a permanent bow, and his features were weathered and leathery. Eva leaned down to speak to him. "I am General Evangeline Booth. How may I help you?"

The old man's eyes lit up, and he reached for her hand and held it tightly as he looked at her face. "Ah, you are the spitting image of your father, that you are," he said. "I heard you would be preaching in this village tonight, and I had to see you with my own eyes. You see, I used to be a lamplighter. And when I was a young man, I happened on your father, William Booth, God rest his soul. He was inspecting a tent recently put up on the Old Quaker burial ground, and something about him drew me over. I talked to him, and I offered to help string the lights in the tent." He stopped and took a long breath. "I'll never forget the words your father said that night."

Eva strained forward, mesmerized by the old man.

"He said to me, 'You mark my words, one day they will be stringing lights just like these around the world.' That's what your father said—those very words."

William Booth's words uttered so long ago were true. Today the Salvation Army spans the globe, reaching out to others with the love of God, the courage of their convictions, and the discipline of good soldiers. The Salvation Army is now established in eighty countries with sixteen thousand evangelical centers and operates more than three thousand social welfare institutions, hospitals, schools, orphanages, homeless shelters, and social service agencies—lights strung around the world.

Bibliography

Booth, William. *In Darkest England and the Way Out.* The Salvation Army, 1984.

Collier, Richard. *The General Next to God: The Story of William and the Salvation Army.* Collins, 1965.

Hattersley, Roy. *Blood and Fire: William and Catherine Booth and Their Salvation Army.* Doubleday, 1999.

Lavine, Sigmund A. *Evangeline Booth: Daughter of Salvation.* Dodd, Mead & Company, 1970.

Steele, Harold C. *I Was a Stranger: The Faith of William Booth, Founder of the Salvation Army.* Exposition Press, 1954.

Wilson, P. W. *General Evangeline Booth of the Salvation Army.* Charles Scribner's Sons, 1948.

About the Authors

Janet and Geoff Benge are a husband and wife writing team with more than thirty years of writing experience. Janet is a former elementary school teacher. Geoff holds a degree in history. Originally from New Zealand, the Benges spent ten years serving with Youth With A Mission. They have two daughters, Laura and Shannon, and an adopted son, Lito. They make their home in the Orlando, Florida, area.

Also from Janet and Geoff Benge…

More adventure-filled biographies for ages 10 to 100!

Christian Heroes: Then and Now

Gladys Aylward: The Adventure of a Lifetime • 978-1-57658-019-6
Nate Saint: On a Wing and a Prayer • 978-1-57658-017-2
Hudson Taylor: Deep in the Heart of China • 978-1-57658-016-5
Amy Carmichael: Rescuer of Precious Gems • 978-1-57658-018-9
Eric Liddell: Something Greater Than Gold • 978-1-57658-137-7
Corrie ten Boom: Keeper of the Angels' Den • 978-1-57658-136-0
William Carey: Obliged to Go • 978-1-57658-147-6
George Müller: Guardian of Bristol's Orphans • 978-1-57658-145-2
Jim Elliot: One Great Purpose • 978-1-57658-146-9
Mary Slessor: Forward into Calabar • 978-1-57658-148-3
David Livingstone: Africa's Trailblazer • 978-1-57658-153-7
Betty Greene: Wings to Serve • 978-1-57658-152-0
Adoniram Judson: Bound for Burma • 978-1-57658-161-2
Cameron Townsend: Good News in Every Language • 978-1-57658-164-3
Jonathan Goforth: An Open Door in China • 978-1-57658-174-2
Lottie Moon: Giving Her All for China • 978-1-57658-188-9
John Williams: Messenger of Peace • 978-1-57658-256-5
William Booth: Soup, Soap, and Salvation • 978-1-57658-258-9
Rowland Bingham: Into Africa's Interior • 978-1-57658-282-4
Ida Scudder: Healing Bodies, Touching Hearts • 978-1-57658-285-5
Wilfred Grenfell: Fisher of Men • 978-1-57658-292-3
Lillian Trasher: The Greatest Wonder in Egypt • 978-1-57658-305-0
Loren Cunningham: Into All the World • 978-1-57658-199-5
Florence Young: Mission Accomplished • 978-1-57658-313-5
Sundar Singh: Footprints Over the Mountains • 978-1-57658-318-0
C.T. Studd: No Retreat • 978-1-57658-288-6
Rachel Saint: A Star in the Jungle • 978-1-57658-337-1
Brother Andrew: God's Secret Agent • 978-1-57658-355-5
Clarence Jones: Mr. Radio • 978-1-57658-343-2
Count Zinzendorf: Firstfruit • 978-1-57658-262-6
John Wesley: The World His Parish • 978-1-57658-382-1
C. S. Lewis: Master Storyteller • 978-1-57658-385-2
David Bussau: Facing the World Head-on • 978-1-57658-415-6
Jacob DeShazer: Forgive Your Enemies • 978-1-57658-475-0
Isobel Kuhn: On the Roof of the World • 978-1-57658-497-2
Elisabeth Elliot: Joyful Surrender • 978-1-57658-513-9
D. L. Moody: Bringing Souls to Christ • 978-1-57658-552-8
Paul Brand: Helping Hands • 978-1-57658-536-8
Dietrich Bonhoeffer: In the Midst of Wickedness • 978-1-57658-713-3
Francis Asbury: Circuit Rider • 978-1-57658-737-9

Samuel Zwemer: The Burden of Arabia • 978-1-57658-738-6
Klaus-Dieter John: Hope in the Land of the Incas • 978-1-57658-826-2
Mildred Cable: Through the Jade Gate • 978-1-57658-886-4
John Flynn: Into the Never Never • 978-1-57658-898-7
Richard Wurmbrand: Love Your Enemies • 978-1-57658-987-8
Charles Mulli: We Are Family • 978-1-57658-894-9
John Newton: Change of Heart • 978-1-57658-909-0
Helen Roseveare: Mama Luka • 978-1-57658-910-6
Norman Grubb: Mission Builder • 978-1-57658-915-1
Albert Schweitzer • 978-1-57658-961-8

Heroes of History

George Washington Carver: From Slave to Scientist • 978-1-883002-78-7
Abraham Lincoln: A New Birth of Freedom • 978-1-883002-79-4
Meriwether Lewis: Off the Edge of the Map • 978-1-883002-80-0
George Washington: True Patriot • 978-1-883002-81-7
William Penn: Liberty and Justice for All • 978-1-883002-82-4
Harriet Tubman: Freedombound • 978-1-883002-90-9
John Adams: Independence Forever • 978-1-883002-50-3
Clara Barton: Courage under Fire • 978-1-883002-51-0
Daniel Boone: Frontiersman • 978-1-932096-09-5
Theodore Roosevelt: An American Original • 978-1-932096-10-1
Douglas MacArthur: What Greater Honor • 978-1-932096-15-6
Benjamin Franklin: Live Wire • 978-1-932096-14-9
Christopher Columbus: Across the Ocean Sea • 978-1-932096-23-1
Laura Ingalls Wilder: A Storybook Life • 978-1-932096-32-3
Orville Wright: The Flyer • 978-1-932096-34-7
Captain John Smith: A Foothold in the New World • 978-1-932096-36-1
Thomas Edison: Inspiration and Hard Work • 978-1-932096-37-8
Alan Shepard: Higher and Faster • 978-1-932096-41-5
Ronald Reagan: Destiny at His Side • 978-1-932096-65-1
Davy Crockett: Ever Westward • 978-1-932096-67-5
Milton Hershey: More Than Chocolate • 978-1-932096-82-8
Billy Graham: America's Pastor • 978-1-62486-024-9
Ben Carson: A Chance at Life • 978-1-62486-034-8
Louis Zamperini: Redemption • 978-1-62486-049-2
Elizabeth Fry: Angel of Newgate • 978-1-62486-064-5
William Wilberforce: Take Up the Fight • 978-1-62486-057-7
William Bradford: Plymouth's Rock • 978-1-62486-092-8
Ernest Shackleton: Going South • 978-1-62486-093-5
Benjamin Rush: The Common Good • 978-1-62486-123-9
Dwight Eisenhower: Supreme Commander • 978-1-62486-142-0